THE
CANNONEERS

GI Life in a World War II Cannon Company

THE
CANNONEERS

GI Life in a World War II Cannon Company

by W. Stanford Smith

with contributions by
Leo J. Machan and Stanley E. Earman

Sunflower University Press ®
1531 Yuma (Box 1009), Manhattan, Kansas 66502-4228

ISBN 0-89745-164-3

Cover: *Armored Field Artillery — WWII,* by Oklahoma artist Joyce Kreafle. Courtesy of United States Field Artillery Association, Fort Sill, Oklahoma. The M-7, 105mm howitzer, motor carriage pictured was a variant of the M-3 tank chassis. It was nicknamed "The Priest" because of its pulpit-like .50-caliber machine-gun ring mount and was one of the most popular weapons of the War.

Edited by Julie Riley Bush

Layout by Lori L. Daniel

*This book
is respectfully dedicated
to the memory
of those members of
Cannon Company, 103rd Infantry,
who gave their lives in service.*

Contents

Foreword

The United States is now commemorating the 50th anniversary of events of World War II. Over a five-year period, 1991-1995, the nation will accord special recognition to those who participated in that allied effort to preserve freedom for all people.

This is the human story of one small unit of the United States Army — men who trained together to build a unit, fought together as a part of the 43rd Infantry Division, and today gather annually in reunions to honor those who gave their lives in service and to renew the friendships forged on the battlefield.

If this narrative does nothing else, it should cause the members of the Cannon Company, 103rd Infantry, to remember with great satisfaction that they faced many hardships with great skill and courage. Every member of the company should feel proud of what they accomplished collectively.

Likewise, the narrative shows my own pride in serving so long as their leader and their friend. Promotion to the rank of major general in the Army many years later could not compare with the satisfaction of serving as commanding officer of the Cannon Company, 103rd Infantry.

This is not a recitation of battles. It is an account of the trials, tribulations, and amusing anecdotes that are typical of the American soldier — Regular, Reservist, National Guardsman, or draftee from civilian life, heroes all.

Preface

"Togetherness" is the best word to describe the men who made up the Cannon Company, 103rd Infantry. Almost 50 years ago they came together from all walks of life, from all parts of the country. Today they are still a unit, maintaining regular contact with each other and assembling in annual reunions each January in Orlando, Florida.

Our Cannon Company was formed specifically to provide a much-needed combat unit for the 103rd Infantry, a regiment of the U.S. Army 43rd Infantry Division. The 103rd Infantry came from Maine. It was one of the three regiments of the 43rd Infantry Division, originally a National Guard division from the New England states of Maine, Connecticut, Vermont, and Rhode Island. The 43rd was one of the first National Guard divisions to be mobilized and deployed to fight in World War II, sent to the Southwest Pacific. We trained with six other recently formed cannon companies, also destined for Army divisions that had already deployed. Since the cannon company was a new idea, it had been added to the standard infantry regimental organization too late for the early deploying divisions.

The mission of the Cannon Company was to provide heavier weapons support for the regimental commander, under his direct control, than did the mortars and other weapons in the old organization structure. The company's principal weapon varied and so did its method of operating, as this story will recount.

The Cannon Company, 103rd Infantry, began with a cadre of 20 men. Most of the rest had been drafted and given 13 weeks of basic training before this assignment. They came willingly to serve their country, training and fighting in the war together. They accepted the harsh discipline of the infantry and learned the intricacies of highly skilled artillery firing.

In telling this story, I have relied greatly on the memories and notes, written long ago, of Leo J. Machan and Stanley E. Earman. When the unit was demobilized in 1945, Leo Machan was the first sergeant. He saved the company guidon, which has been the rallying point for the members at the annual reunions. Stanley "Shorty" Earman is the driving force in locating long-lost members and enlisting their interest in the reunions through a Cannon Company newsletter, *Fire Mission!*

For most of the war, I was the company commander. This is our story.

W. Stanford Smith
Major General, USA-Ret.
Captain, Infantry 1943-1945

Chapter 1

The Coming Together

The nearest thing to a birth date for the Cannon Company, 103rd Infantry, was 24 December 1942. On that date, a cadre of 20 men assembled at Fort Lewis, Washington, and departed at 1900 hours by a two-and-a-half-ton truck for the railroad station in Seattle. The men knew very well that it was Christmas Eve and that they would celebrate Christmas Day on the train; but it would not be much of a celebration. The going-away parties at Fort Lewis had left many of the Cannoneers (as they shall be called throughout this account) ill, and they did not enjoy the ride at all.

These 20 men from the 33rd Division, Fort Lewis, led by Lieutenant Rix Maurer, arrived on 26 December at Paso Robles, California, where they were met by Army medical personnel who looked down throats, examined chests, and, finding nothing dangerous, let them board trucks for Camp Roberts, California.

Camp Roberts was organized and equipped as an Infantry Replacement Training Center with barracks and facilities to provide basic training for draftees. This meant that the hardy band of Cannoneers wound up in pyramidal tents in the West Garrison of the post. The tents had Sibley stoves — small, crude heating devices that burned wood — but no fuel and no lights. One group got chewed out by the Fire Guard for lighting a fire in the stove, but the Officer of the Day never found out who had torn up the wooden floor for kindling.

Events over the next year showed that the people in charge of Camp Roberts were never certain about the status of the new cannon companies or their responsibility for training or command. Cannon company commanders essentially had no higher command to report to, thus leaving them with more authority than almost any other company-level commander in the Army. This turned out to have many advantages when I arrived on the scene later.

On 27 December 1942, the 103rd Infantry cadre had its first formation as a unit:

Cannon Company, 103rd Infantry

Headquarters Platoon
First Sergeant — John Smurlo
Company Clerk — Stanley Korman
Supply Sergeant — J. P. Kulawik
Supply Clerk — Virgil M. Dilly
Armorer — Richard A. Wall
Mess Sergeant — Chester L. Dilbeck
Motor Sergeant — George W. Harper
Communications Sergeant — Lee R. Schmidt
Fire Direction Center — Clarence H. Haug
Fire Direction Center — Edward W. Juresic
Mail Clerk — Frank Mattingly

1st Platoon
Platoon Sergeant — Kenneth W. Nelson
Section Chief — Fred A. Gustafson
Section Chief — Vincent Gagliano

2nd Platoon
Platoon Sergeant — Clarence B. Waldhier
Section Chief — Sam J. Terracina
Section Chief — Theodore J. Jackson

3rd Platoon
Platoon Sergeant —Leo J. Machan
Section Chief — Otto G. Hof
Section Chief — William Kopy

Training Begins
Over what would have been the New Year's holiday, 1943, the cadre was put to work doing menial chores — sweeping, KP duty, and the like. Even the senior enlisted cadre members participated, as the company had no privates yet. The company was moved to the East Garrison of Camp Roberts to erect

its own "tent city" at the south end of the post, far from whatever amenities were available to others at the camp.

A few carpenters put up wooden frames for the company's pyramidal tents, and the troops nailed down the floors and set tents on the frames. Sibley stoves were installed; the weather, though warm in the daytime, was cold at night. The troops had a few other duties — digging drainage ditches, hauling gravel for the company street, building walkways across the ditches, hauling firewood, and raking, sweeping, and cleaning the camp area.

Cooks joined the unit as the first additions to the cadre, a welcome addition as chow at the time was reported to be "terrible." Then, just after the first of the new year, the first two privates arrived to join the company. Stephens and Garrett were welcomed and placed immediately on KP. Three more officers soon arrived to join Lieutenant Rix Maurer: Lieutenant Clinton F. Lee, Lieutenant Leo J. Canjar, and Lieutenant Ralph Gribben.

The cadre began training for the mission of the Cannon Company. Most of the men had come from field artillery, and the Cannon Company method of operation was to be somewhat different — just how different, we learned much later.

The official Table of Organization and Equipment (TO&E) of the infantry cannon company provided that its principal weapon would be an infantry adaptation of the field-artillery-towed 105-millimeter howitzer. It was essentially the same as the standard 105-mm towed howitzer in the artillery battalions that normally supported infantry regiments, but it had a shorter barrel (which presumably increased its mobility) that somewhat reduced its range and accuracy. Most of the officers had attended a six-week course at Fort Benning, Georgia, to learn the equipment and tactics of the cannon company, but we never saw the short-barrel 105-mm howitzer after we left Fort Benning.

Instead, the cannon companies at Camp Roberts received 75-millimeter pack howitzers rather than the 105-mm. These weapons were designed to be carried on the backs of mules in mountain fighting. They had wooden wheels and iron tires when issued to us, but the plan was to have them converted to "high-speed wheels" with rubber tires. That did happen, but "high speed" is a somewhat exaggerated term. The wheels were mounted in such a way that turns could be made only on an extremely wide arc. Speed was thus severely limited.

The New CO Arrives

Upon commissioning in the infantry, I was assigned in June 1941 to train recruits at the Infantry Replacement Training Center, Camp Croft, South Carolina. When my request in 1942 for transfer to a combat unit was turned down, I thought I was doomed to train recruits for the duration of the war. I then got a two-week leave, married the "girl of my dreams," Martha Cooper, on 4 October 1942, and returned to Camp Croft to find orders sending me to something called the Cannon Company Officers Course at Fort Benning, Georgia.

We drove to Fort Benning where I joined about 100 other infantry lieutenants in a course designed to qualify us for duty with something most of us had never heard of — an infantry cannon company. A new TO&E provided one such company in each infantry regiment to give heavier weapons support under the regimental commander's direct control than did the existing heavy weapons companies armed with 81-millimeter mortars and machine guns.

We were taught the tactics of rapid forward deployment to keep up with advancing rifle troops. We went through many training exercises and finally were pronounced ready for assignment to cannon companies. Many regiments had deployed to Europe and the Pacific before cannon companies became part of the TO&E. This mean that some companies would be organized and trained in the U.S. and join their regiments after completion of training, but I did not know this at the time.

The course ended in mid-February 1943. After some paperwork shuffling by the various headquarters involved, I received orders to Cannon Company, 103rd Infantry, Camp Roberts, California, with travel by privately owned conveyance authorized (TPA). Knowing nothing about the 43rd Division or the 103rd Infantry, I thought I would find the regiment at Camp Roberts. Little did I know.

Martha and I set out in our 1941 Chevrolet to cross the country. Army regulations then required individuals traveling by automobile who were on duty time (not on leave) to cover at least 250 miles per day. This was easy, and we took advantage of the opportunity to see the sights by driving 400 or 500 miles per day, then stopping at places such as the Grand Canyon and Carlsbad Caverns. We made the trip well within the authorized time.

In due course, I arrived at the Camp Roberts Military Police Gate where I asked for the location of the 103rd Infantry. The MP gave me a blank stare, said there was no such unit on the post, then went inside and made a few phone calls. He came back with only the laconic comment that the unit I was looking for was in "them tents." I did not consider that an auspicious arrival, nor was I greatly encouraged when I found that the troops were, indeed, in "them tents" surrounded by muddy ditches.

I don't remember who gave me the news that I was the company commander because I was the senior first lieutenant of the five then assigned to the 103rd Infantry Cannon Company. However, I took command of the company on 19 March 1943.

In my first week of command, I learned many things. I found that we had a weapon — the 75-mm pack howitzer — that I had never seen and knew

The 75-millimeter pack howitzer used by the Cannoneers for training in California but never in combat.

nothing about. And I discovered that I had no effective higher command to report to, thus leaving me with more authority than I had expected. But I thought that that was a dandy situation.

As I met and got acquainted with the cadre, I was pleased to find some who seemed to be top-quality NCOs, but I also suspected that some had been chosen "out" of their old units rather than selected for a possible promotion. However, I would assess and deal with that situation later. I soon decided that the level of discipline and physical conditioning of the unit left something to be desired. And training on the howitzers was uncertain and still in its early stages.

But all these things could be corrected. They presented a challenge that I welcomed. I liked the men and was confident that we could build an effective combat unit. One of my first decisions as Cannon Company CO was to select Private Harold W. Hovdenes as my jeep driver. He remained my driver, and close friend, throughout my tenure. I called him "Pete" and still do, although none of his relatives or friends use that nickname.

Believing that we would go to war armed with the strange 75-mm pack howitzer (an assumption that later turned out to be false), I calculated that we would face many difficulties getting them into firing positions. The guns were towed behind ¾-ton trucks, which I knew would not be able to reach firing positions in jungle and semi-jungle terrain. I thought that a certain amount of manhandling would be required. Leo Machan, then sergeant, and Stan Earman, then corporal, comment on that:

Machan: *The 75-mm mountain gun should have been left in the mountains. We had to load the damned thing piece by piece into a trailer. It was probably the cause of more hernias than weight lifting.*

Earman: *We trained on the 75-mm howitzer, having previously trained on the 105- and 155-mm howitzers. We must have assembled and taken them apart a thousand times. We dragged them up mountains piece by piece.*

But everyone survived these ordeals, and if we had gone to war with these weapons, we would have been capable of using them almost anywhere. However, all of us were eventually glad that we had something better when we did go into combat.

The Fillers Arrive

In January, two months before I joined the company as CO, the men the company needed to fill to required strength began arriving. The first group came from infantry basic training, not what the Cannon Company needed. Some were kept; most were not. The next group came from field artillery

The Cannon Company officers: Captain W. Stanford Smith, Lieutenant Leo J. Canjar, Lieutenant Charles Rice, Lieutenant Rix Maurer, and Lieutenant Clinton F. Lee.

basic training, and that was what the company needed most — men to form the six gun crews.

Overall, we were fortunate with the caliber of men assigned to the company. Three came from Officer Candidate Training School; Stanley Earman was one of these. But he said that he and the two others had dropped out "because we didn't care for methods the officers were required to use." He was probably referring to the discipline that officers were expected to mete out; many men did not like that aspect of the job. Ken Crossman and Warren Evrard joined us at the same time. These three proved to be valuable members of the company.

We gained another important addition about this time. Lieutenant Ralph Gribben had asked for a transfer to another cannon company that was commanded by a friend of his. I offered no objection and was greatly pleased to get his replacement, Second Lieutenant Ray Moss, a field artillery officer. He brought to us great expertise in employment of the howitzer. Gradually the company grew to required TO&E strength.

Training areas were limited at Camp Roberts, so effort was concentrated on gun drill, selection and occupation of gun positions, map reading, motor maintenance, and, of course, physical training (hikes) and close-order drill. As an infantry officer, I had been imbued with the importance of discipline and physical conditioning. I have no doubt that the men did not always appreciate the stress on long hikes, but I believe they understood the reasons. Some overnight bivouacs were arranged along with motor-march convoy training using our 20-odd vehicles.

Rumors began to circulate that we would be going overseas soon, or that we would be going to Texas, or that we would be moved to the boondocks somewhere in California. The latter proved true.

Chapter 2

Camp Pleyto

To acquire terrain for proper training, we moved in May 1943 to Camp Pleyto, California, an old CCC camp on Hunter Liggett Military Reservation. We were thus located some 30 miles from Camp Roberts and, more importantly, about 40 miles from Paso Robles, the nearest city and the place where some company members had wives or girlfriends. I took that into consideration on weekends when passes were given out.

Camp Pleyto must have been a one-of-a-kind military training site. We arrived to find tarpaper barracks, pit latrines, and cold-water showers. But we did have our own mess hall and a kitchen crew that could do justice to issued rations. After a couple of weeks, we managed to get hot water for the showers.

Field training could then be conducted in earnest — and it was.

Machan: *We were introduced to the 9-mile hike in an hour and 50 minutes with full field pack and weapon. It was hell on men with short legs; they had to run most of the way. We had a 20-mile hike scheduled on one of the hottest days of 1943. With no packs, just pistol belt, weapon and steel helmet, we were to complete this hike in six hours. As the day stretched on and the temperature rose, the column grew longer. Men were dropping out and trying to catch up when they were able. A canteen of water didn't last too long. Many men got sick after too many salt tablets. Only 15 men arrived back in camp with Lieutenant Moss and the main body. Two men were hospitalized for heat exhaustion.*

I learned something from that experience but not what the men thought I had learned: I concluded that the troops needed more physical training in the form of a few more hikes. I also saw a need for discipline in the use of salt tablets.

Other training continued with steady progress in the gun sections, with emphasis on training of section chiefs and gun crews in the rapid execution of the fire mission commands. We did many hundreds of "dry runs" in paralleling the battery (ensuring that all weapons were pointed in parallel lines in the general direction of the target area) and laying the guns on fire commands to be checked at each stage by the officers.

This training was sometimes interrupted by calls to send our troops out to fight forest fires within the reservation. That interruption could occur only if the administrative brass hats at Camp Roberts could reach someone in authority in our company, and they became less successful as our training advanced. I saw training as a higher priority than fighting forest fires, even though we had started a few ourselves when we used live ammunition. Even when the brass could reach me — or the Charge of Quarters after hours — the company men had a system of their own for avoiding this job. One man would hang around the Orderly Room and listen for the phone call, then alert the troops so they could hide. Favorite places were under the barracks and behind the latrine; for some reason, no one thought of looking there. But a few men were usually caught and became "volunteer fire-fighters."

This was not the only problem I had with our so-called higher headquarters, which carried the name Headquarters, Special Troops. I never did feel that anyone there understood what we were doing. When they tried to manage our training, the results were not good. One day all seven cannon companies at Camp Pleyto were scheduled for live firing with our 75-mm howitzers. The major who had the title of Operations Officer (S-3) simply drew seven parallel lines on a map and assigned an area to each of the cannon companies. I took one look at our area and told him that we could not fire there because of the presence of many civilian telephone lines. His reply, in almost exact words, was, "Captain, you will do as you are told."

So, we did as we were told and shot out the telephone connections between Los Angeles and San Francisco. All hell broke loose then as to who was responsible for that fiasco, but I didn't give a damn.

Leo Machan recalls another snafu that had better results:

Machan: *Third platoon was in firing position with Lieutenant Leo Canjar as Forward Observer (FO). He called, "Cease firing, end of mission," which does* not *mean that it's time to pack everything up. But the communications man misunderstood and gave me "CSMO" — Close Station, March Order, which means it's time to go home, so we tore down to move out. But then here* came the command, *"Fire mission."* *It was a scramble to re-lay the guns with lots of delay. I don't remember what kind of excuse I gave Lieutenant Canjar, who got onto me for the screw-up. That evening I held a class in telephone procedure.*

All infantry troops have to train for combat in cities, even cannon companies. A town setup had been built for this kind of training with many booby traps laid in the buildings, and the Cannoneers practiced fighting. The men seemed to enjoy this exercise, but it also led to incidents like this one:

Machan: *A few boxes of booby traps fell into the hands of the troops, and no place was safe. Men were afraid to open doors or to lift lids in the latrines. It was a lot of fun, and fortunately no one was injured. Even Captain Smith's desk was booby-trapped. When he sat down and pulled open the drawer of his desk, there was an explosion under his feet. The booby trap was under the floor, and the trip wire ran to the back of the desk drawer. At first he was pissed off, but in a few minutes he laughed with the rest of us. But the next day there was a notice on the bulletin board informing us to turn in all booby traps. That noon the door to the mess hall was booby-trapped.*

There was not much entertainment at Camp Pleyto, but volleyball and softball were possible. Leo Machan tried umpiring the softball games but caught so much hell from both teams that he gave it up as a bad job and decided against a postwar career as a major league umpire.

Rifle-range firing was almost like entertainment for some, especially those who had grown up in the country. Sergeants Leonard Schoneman and Leo Machan competed each day with a bottle of beer bet on each of 20 shots. At the end of the two weeks, Machan owed Schoneman seven bottles of beer. We would hike out to the range in the morning, would have noon chow brought to us, and would hike back in the evening. We had trucks we could use, but I saw this as another opportunity for a seven-mile hike.

We Make Some Changes

Changes are inevitable in any organization. In a military unit preparing for combat, the commander must shape a leadership team which he thinks will result in success. As commander of what the Army termed a "separate company," I had far more authority to make promotions and reductions than a company commander in a battalion or regiment.

I decided that I needed a first sergeant in whom I could have full confidence and who would have the same confidence in me. I selected Kenneth W. Nelson, who was platoon sergeant of the first platoon. I was also not satisfied with the efficiency of the company supply operations, so I promoted Virgil

Dilly to supply sergeant. I sent the incumbents in those two positions to higher headquarters for immediate reassignment. I did not make these decisions lightly; I gave them a lot of thought and consulted the other officers. But they were my decisions, and I never regretted them.

Virgil Dilly told me later that when he received the message to report to me, he was "quaking in his boots," wondering what he had done to get into trouble. He was surprised by the appointment and the promotion. He was a fine person and always justified my confidence in him.

Other changes came later, but these two contributed greatly to the efficient operations of the company and, in my judgment, eventually to success in combat.

Advanced Training

By June it was time for the kind of training that would get our company in a condition referred to today as "combat-ready." Isolated as we were at Camp Pleyto, we had access to few training aids, but we did have models of the Browning Automatic Rifle (BAR) and of the lensatic compass.

Anticipating jungle patrol operations, I conducted classes for everyone in use of the compass, map reading, and cross-country navigation. The men learned well, but, as in all such training, some got lost during the field exercise. The same thing had occurred when officers and officer candidates took similar instruction at The Infantry School, so I was not discouraged.

As a kind of test, we laid out a cross-country compass march. This was not a spectacular success, as one of the platoons found out where the course ended. One section just skipped all legs of the course and went directly to the final assembly area. However, they miscalculated, because they arrived too soon for them to have covered the whole course.

Then we had a test to see whether the men could handle the howitzers if trucks were not available or could not operate in rough terrain.

Machan: *One hot day the CO decided we should manhandle the guns into position. We drove out to the area he picked — a nice long hill, fairly steep. We tried to make it easier by taking the top plate and barrel off the guns, then pulling them to the top, but we were getting nowhere fast. Cursing the guns, the CO, Camp Pleyto, and the Army didn't help at all. Finally, I put a guard on Kopy's gun and had the whole platoon drag Sergeant Hof's gun up the hill. We used all the prolongs — long ropes — and one set of truck tire chains and finally reached the top. Getting back down wasn't much easier, but we got the job done. We were lucky that no one was hurt.*

There are a few things everyone must do before deployment overseas; one of those is chemical warfare training in use of the gas mask. We set up a small gas chamber for that purpose. After a one-hour lecture, everyone had to enter the gas chamber, put on his mask, and then exit. Breathing tear gas is one of those experiences every Army veteran remembers. However, despite regulations requiring us to carry gas masks at all times, we discarded them overseas. We did not expect the Japanese to use chemical warfare, and neither did our intelligence officers. A few men did use the covers to carry small treasured items.

I have already mentioned that I did not ignore the plight of the men being in such an isolated location as Camp Pleyto. I tried to be generous with weekend passes and usually allowed them to take a two-and-a-half-ton truck to Camp Roberts from where they could get transportation to Paso Robles. But even this presented difficulties, because invariably several thousand men were looking for rides from Camp Roberts to Paso Robles.

Machan: *One Saturday afternoon, the CO put me in charge of the truck. Instead of stopping at Camp Roberts, I went on into Paso Robles and let off the men I had with me from Camp Pleyto. When we crossed the intersection as we returned to Roberts, Captain Smith was standing there. He was looking straight at me, so all I could do was salute and keep going. Monday morning I expected a royal ass-chewing, but the CO never mentioned the incident. You can be sure I never asked to take a truck to town again.*

One of the lieutenants, when he had Officer of the Day duty (entailing no specific responsibilities), had a habit of sacking out on a certain enlisted man's bunk. The man didn't like this, so he eventually gave the sleeping lieutenant a "shoe-polish hot foot," which caused a pretty good burn. The guilty party always referred to this as a "training accident."

Another time an incident occurred that caused me to impose severe "company punishment" on one of our men. I had received an envelope addressed to me from the War Department, Washington, DC. Inside was a letter written to Mrs. Roosevelt complaining that "my company commander is so mean he won't give me a furlough to go home to see about my farm. He is so mean he won't even give me a three-day pass." The letter had been endorsed by the War Department and by each succeeding level in the chain of command with the simple notation, "Forwarded as a matter pertaining to your command." I called the man in and asked him, "Who is your company commander?" He replied, "You are, sir," upon which I berated him and assigned him the maximum seven days of company punishment, during which time he was to clean all our field kitchens — a most disagreeable task. I also required him to report to the Charge of Quarters every hour on the hour, from the time he woke up until he went to bed. Later I was told that his wife had actually written the letter without his knowledge, but I am not convinced that that was the truth.

As our training advanced satisfactorily to platoon and company level tactical exercises, we went through the required tests to see whether we were "ready for combat." On about the second trial, we satisfied the umpires, who, I suspected, knew little of what they were seeing. Officially, we were ready to go overseas. But something important remained to be accomplished: We needed to prepare all our equipment for shipment. This meant making waterproof boxes for every piece of unit equipment and sealing and labeling the boxes with our shipment number: 6898-B. We were issued everything needed to make the boxes — lumber, nails, a banding machine, and the banding material.

Making the boxes and doing it properly was such an enormous task that I assigned the entire company to this mission. Each gun crew and each platoon would make its own boxes, and the same was true of company headquarters personnel. So, at this point we had no training schedule. Everyone was occupied with the preparation for overseas movement.

As luck would have it, some higher headquarters picked that week to send an inspector to visit us. A major, spiffy in his uniform, arrived at our tarpaper shack Orderly Room and confronted Sergeant Nelson and me in our grubby fatigues. His first words were, "Let me see your training schedule." When I indicated that we didn't have one, he interrupted with, "Don't you know you are required to have a training schedule?"

I pointed out that everyone was making boxes for overseas shipment, but he again insisted that we had to have a training schedule. At that I replied, "Okay, I will make one. It will only take a minute. It will say, 'All personnel — making boxes.'"

He walked around the company area a few minutes, saw the men making boxes, decided I was a hopeless case, and went away. I never heard anymore about that inspection.

Back to Camp Roberts

Some time in the month of September 1943 we were deemed fully trained, so we moved back to Camp Roberts. This time we were billeted in standard two-story wooden barracks. We drew additional equipment that we would need in the Southwest Pacific — a second canteen for every man, wire cutters, map cases, machetes, and one flare gun per platoon. We went through equipment inspections and dental checks, and our immunizations were brought up to date.

Our orders were delayed several times, so we had the opportunity to grant leaves to everyone. We only needed to know how to reach them in case of sudden orders, and that never happened; we were delayed up until Christmas.

One of the highlights of this period was a gala Christmas dinner in the company mess hall to which the wives of all officers and enlisted men were invited. Everyone agreed our cooks did a fine job, and it was an occasion we would remember for a long time. My wife recalls:

Martha Smith: *That Christmas Day was hot at Camp Roberts, dusty and dry. The mess hall was crowded with handsome soldiers and a handful of mystified wives wearing festive dresses. Red, white, and blue streamers decorated the room; a small U.S. flag (48 stars then) was a table favor at each place. The standard turkey dinner was served. After the meal, there was mingling and singing of carols. As the holiday happiness grew, it seemed so did the crowd. Ruth Machan and I backed ourselves against a wall, wide-eyed, to view the frolic. We sang a little, but mostly I think we gave each other comfort. Every person present was young, happy, and healthy — except even then the wives were frightened of what the future held. Maybe the men were as well.*

Finally, we got our orders and departed Camp Roberts on the evening of 28 December for Camp Stoneman near San Francisco from where we would depart to go "somewhere in the South Pacific."

Chapter 3

Camp Stoneman

Leaving behind our wives, sweethearts, other friends, and privately owned automobiles, we made our way without incident to Camp Stoneman, California — a dreary place — with the sole purpose of receiving and shipping out to the war in the Pacific all those units and individuals deemed ready for their overseas missions. The Cannon Company, 103rd Infantry, was in that category; however, we did not have high enough priority to get us onto an immediate outbound troop ship.

Upon arrival at Camp Stoneman, we were again given superficial medical checks, which consisted of looking down our throats and at our chests. We were billeted in standard barracks, ate in a consolidated mess hall that fed all us "transients," and went through another inspection of our clothing and personal equipment (our unit equipment was in the boxes we had laboriously built).

When a delay of some days was apparent, the wives of several enlisted men came to the San Francisco area, along with my wife and Lieutenant Rix Maurer's wife. (The other officers were not married.) There was no reason to deprive these men of the opportunity to be with their spouses again before departure, so I followed a generous pass policy. I think the men appreciated this and that it helped cement the feeling of "togetherness" that still prevails today.

Training facilities at Camp Stoneman were extremely limited, but we needed to keep busy, so we used whatever was available. We had some classes in the barracks and showed some training films. We ran the post obstacle course frequently, sometimes more than once a day, and worked over the bayonet course pretty heavily, almost destroying some of the targets, although we were confident we would not be doing much bayonet fighting. Little did we know then that we would be called on more than once to fight as a rifle company. Of course, we did not need training facilities to make hikes, so the Cannon Company made a nine-mile hike every Saturday morning while we were at Camp Stoneman.

Part of our physical training was climbing cargo nets like those we would use later to make amphibious landings. Wall scaling was also part of this course. Leo Machan remembers one sergeant, who was a bit on the heavy side, as the one who had the most difficulty getting over the wall. However, I remember that I had just as much trouble as the sergeant did. I hated that this made me look weak to the troops, but wall scaling was not one of my talents. Fortunately, we never had to scale a single wall during our entire experience in combat.

Our troops played some football at Camp Stoneman. In one of those games, Stan Earman severely injured his ankle. It was x-rayed on sick call and no breaks were found, but he was confined to quarters. The medics recommended that Earman remain at Camp Stoneman, but he wanted to stay with us; I certainly wanted him also. Sergeant Clarence Cochran and Private Frank Chea carried him aboard the troop ship when we eventually sailed.

At this final stage before departure, I was determined that every member of the company would go. There would be no exceptions for any reason whatever. But one of our men apparently had been given advice by some "guardhouse lawyer" that he was entitled to have his own doctor or dentist take care of any physical problem before going overseas. He complained of a toothache and demanded the right to go to his own dentist somewhere back in the Middle West. I remember summoning Sergeant Clarence Waldhier, a big, tough platoon sergeant, and giving him instructions to take this man directly to the Army dentist and to tell the dentist that I wanted his toothache resolved immediately. Waldhier took my instructions literally: He drove the jeep directly across the parade field to the medical center, not bothering to use the road. The soldier got his toothache treated, and both of us dropped the subject.

In another case, two men had a bit more serious problem. On a pass into town, a corporal and a private first class had been invited by a traveling salesman to ride with him to Stockton where they were sure to find "a lot of fun" because they were in uniform and there were so few soldiers there. The salesman was right; they did have fun with two young lady friends there. As they told it later, they realized about 0400 that they had urgent need to get back to Camp Stoneman. Having no transportation, they decided to "borrow" the car belonging to one of the girls. They hot-wired it but never got started, as the local police had spotted them. The young lady declined to press charges and asked that they be let go. Instead, the police summoned the Military Police, and our two Cannoneers wound up in the hands of the Camp Stoneman provost marshal. A court-martial was duly scheduled. Obviously, this meant that they would be convicted and confined, thus missing shipment with us. I intervened with the provost marshal, insisted that they be remanded to my custody, took them back to the company, and reduced them in rank to private. Today, one of the men remembers it as a last-minute reprieve and insists that I had to take them directly to the ship, which was ready to sail. To this day he suspects that one reason for my intervention was that he, the company clerk, was one of only two members of the company who could type. The other one was me.

To the best of my recollection, we took the ferry to Oakland and boarded the *Boschfontein* on Valentine's Day, 14 February 1944. As usual, the Cannon Company made a move on a special occasion.

Chapter 4

The *Boschfontein* and New Caledonia

The *Boschfontein* was an old and dirty Dutch ship pressed into service as a troop carrier. Its officers were Dutch, its crew Indonesian. It carried a small U.S. Navy gun crew to man two five-inch guns and four .50-caliber machine guns. It is highly unlikely that they could have repelled any serious attack.

I was struck immediately by the enormous difference between the quarters assigned to officers and those to the enlisted men. I shared a small stateroom with three other officers, which was small but absolutely spacious compared with the troop billeting. None of our officers was comfortable about that, but it was beyond our control. Our troops were billeted in the hold in bunks stacked four high, all jammed together. This is not a good setup when men start getting seasick.

It is common for ships to encounter high waves as they exit San Francisco Bay. Ours was no exception, and the predictable result ensued: Almost everyone started getting sick. The sleeping quarters became a stinking mess as the latrines overflowed onto the decks. Some men were so ill that they just lay in all that filth.

I have only the word of our men for the above description. I had felt my responsibility and started to go visit our troops, but First Sergeant Kenneth Nelson insisted that I not go below. He argued that there was nothing I could accomplish, that the men already knew my concern for their welfare, and that the only result would be that I would become as sick as most of them were. He won the argument, and I stayed topside. For some reason I did not get seasick.

Sergeant Frank Davenport claimed he had a system to avoid seasickness.

He had been in the Merchant Marine and had learned that the way to beat it was to take a dose of Epsom salts before sailing. He said he never got sick. But 15 minutes later he threw up on Sergeant Clarence Waldhier's back. Sergeant Vincent Gagliano was also extremely ill. Some of the men slept on the deck to get fresh air and avoid the pollution below.

After we got out to sea, the sickness abated, but life for troops on a transport is never pleasant. The men were fed three meals per day, such as they were, at stand-up tables using their own mess gear. Breakfast was always hard boiled eggs, cold cereal with powdered milk, bread, and coffee. Once in a while they had oatmeal, which our men said looked and tasted like cement. Dinner in the middle of the day was usually hot dogs with sauerkraut and boiled potatoes; supper was not much different. Leo Machan reported that once they had greasy pork chops, and half the troops were sick again.

Drinking water for the troops was turned on at only 0600 to 0630 and 1800 to 1830. If you didn't fill your canteens, you went thirsty. Cold saltwater showers were the norm on the ship, even for officers who otherwise were treated the same as the ship's officers. On one occasion in warm weather, it started to rain, and many men went for soap, stripped on the deck, and lathered. Then suddenly it stopped raining. A few naughty words ensued.

As the ship moved farther south, the weather became so hot that the sleeping quarters became almost unbearable. Men stripped to their shorts and sat around their bunks sweating — a foretaste of the tropics. In the daytime the crew rigged a windsock down the hatch, which helped some, but at night with the total blackout, the hatches were shut down, and it was just HOT.

We had regular lifeboat drills, and the crew frequently practiced manning their positions in case of an emergency, but these were just exercises; we were never fired on. We did not have great confidence in the lifeboats or the life preservers. We doubted that the lifeboats' capacity equalled the number of people on board. Some of the men even threw life preservers into the ocean and watched them sink.

For exercise we scheduled some physical training on deck. One morning the crew was rigging some tackle on a mast and dropped a block. It just missed Lieutenant Leo Canjar, who was conducting the PT. That ended the PT for the rest of the voyage.

For entertainment, there was gambling wherever a blanket could be spread. It took the form of poker, blackjack, and craps. Some men played pinochle or hearts. A movie was available 24 hours a day in a compartment that would hold about 40 men but was like a steam bath. The ship also had a library with a good selection, including late best-sellers. In addition, there were boxing matches on deck, with the winner getting to take a freshwater shower in the crew's quarters. A small Post Exchange on the ship offered cigarettes at 45 cents per carton along with such items as fig newtons, Zig Zag candy bars,

Boxing matches entertained troops on the *Boschfontein* en route to the South Pacific.

gum, toilet articles, towels, and chewing tobacco.

Lieutenant Frank DeCorso, a sax player who had once played with Charlie Barnett, formed a band to entertain the troops. Everything they played seemed to sound like "Honeysuckle Rose," which was Barnett's theme song. Other musicians included Don Campbell on drums.

Rumors abounded that we would join a convoy south of Hawaii, but that never happened, and we continued on our merry way. On 23 February, everyone was duly inducted into the "Order of Neptune," a status conferred upon those crossing the equator by ship for the first time. The crew set up a canvas water tank with a plank. King Neptune and Davy Jones took charge with their cohorts, grabbing men out of the crowd for formal initiation. Some got syrup and oatmeal shampoos; some were painted with Mercurochrome. All were blindfolded and had to walk the plank. Everyone received a certificate of crossing.

The long sea journey ended on 6 March 1944 when we landed at Nouméa, New Caledonia, an island in the South Pacific. U.S. military installations on New Caledonia were primarily a staging area to receive units and individuals and send them along to their destinations, mostly the islands where fighting was going on to the north. We soon found out that we were the exception. The 43rd Division was in New Zealand, which is south of New Caledonia. They were enjoying a rest period after their bloody battles at New Georgia, Munda, and nearby islands in the Pacific, so we would be going south to join them. Tokyo Rose, the Japanese radio propaganda voice, had given the division the nickname of the "Munda Butchers," proudly accepted by its members.

A staging area requires a lot of work details, and the Cannon Company was called upon to furnish its share. One afternoon when a group of our men returned from a work detail, I asked them what they had been doing. I was surprised when they answered that they had been dumping overcoats into the ocean. They had been loading boxes of overcoats on a barge, going out to sea, and dumping them overboard.

The next day I got a phone call from the camp supply office telling me to have our men turn in their overcoats. I refused to do so, as I figured the coats would simply be thrown in the ocean. I tried to explain that we were not going north but instead were going south where it might be pretty cold, as we were in the southern hemisphere. We might need the coats later, and we could always throw them away or give them to somebody else if we didn't.

New Caledonia provided our men with the introduction to the kind of food we would be eating for a long time — Spam, powdered eggs, dehydrated potatoes, and powdered milk. When we finally got our own mess equipment, our cooks became quite adept at turning these items into edible meals.

There was not much to do on New Caledonia. We did some physical training, but mostly the men were free to explore the island or go fishing when

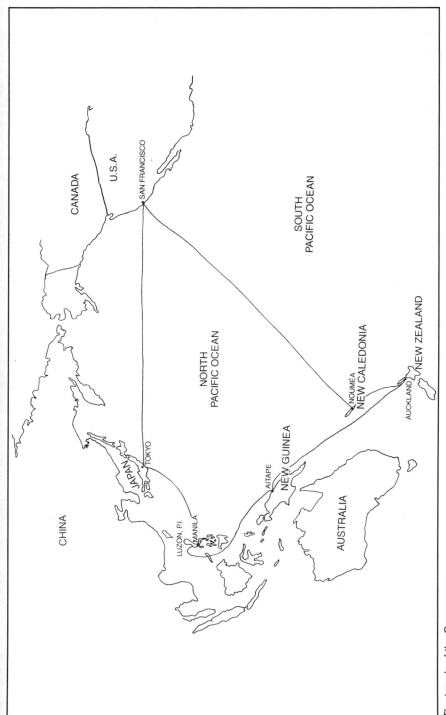

The travels of the Cannoneers.

they were not on work details. Our stay was mercifully short, as we sailed on 25 March 1944 on the USS *Tryon* heading for New Zealand.

Chapter 5

New Zealand

We arrived at Auckland, New Zealand, on 29 March. Our three months there were eventful. At last we had a higher headquarters that we could identify, and I had a real boss. The rest of the division was there for relaxation and recreation, and our men were able to take advantage of that circumstance. We could forget about Spam and powdered eggs for a while, as beef, lamb, milk, and ice cream were plentiful.

A major development was that we never saw the 75-mm pack howitzers that we had trained on at Camp Roberts and Camp Pleyto. Instead, we received the M-7, a self-propelled 105-mm howitzer mounted on a tank chassis, open at the top with a ring mount for a .50-caliber machine gun. This was a formidable weapon, and in addition to learning the details of the weapon itself, including the sights and laying the battery, we had to train drivers and devise tactics for employment that surely would be different from the towed 75-mm howitzer. We received six M-7s to replace our six pack howitzers. We no longer needed the ¾-ton trucks to tow the guns, but we kept as many as regiment would allow, figuring we would always need trucks wherever we went.

We were welcomed by our regimental commander, Colonel Joseph P. Cleland, a West Point graduate who had been Division Chief of Staff before taking command of the 103rd Infantry. He was obviously an ambitious Regular Army officer. He was eager to learn about the M-7, but I had to learn about it myself before I could brief him. This weapon had never been mentioned when I was trained at Fort Benning to become a cannon company officer.

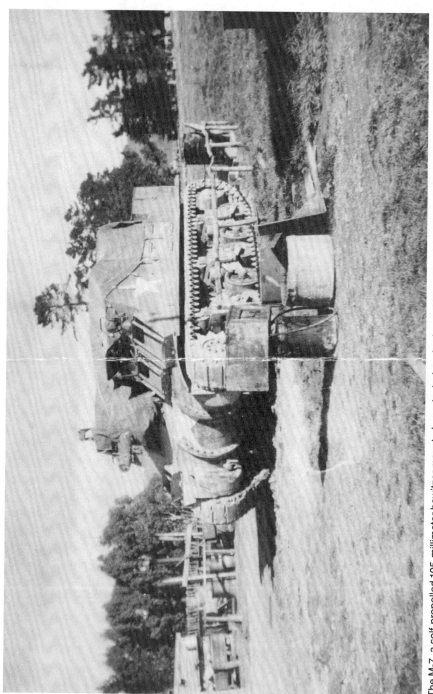

The M-7, a self-propelled 105-millimeter howitzer mounted on a tank chassis along with a .50-caliber machine gun. The Cannon Company took six of these into combat.

We were billeted in the small town of Warkworth, north of Auckland, in the Rodney Fair Grounds. We had a building with an open side for our kitchen, and three small wooden huts. I took one for my quarters, and the other four officers shared the other two. The rest of the company was in pyramidal tents. The weather was pleasant and the food was good.

Warkworth offered some diversion for our troops. It had a hardware store, grocery, church, and one bar, which was open only two hours each evening. That resulted in a mad scramble for drinks. Anyone who got more than one considered himself lucky. The troops customarily walked to town, about two miles from our camp. Three of our men bought motorcycles, but they made a terrible, objectionable racket in the company area. In due course some unidentified party or parties told them to get rid of the bikes, and they did.

There was no officers' club or other special facility for the officers, but the NCOs almost had an NCO club. It just didn't work out, as Leo Machan explains:

Machan: *A local man wanted to start an NCO club in the big tin building at the fair grounds. He held a meeting in the town hall, and we voted him in as manager. Dues weren't much, and he promised whiskey and beer. It was a place for us to hang out, and we played cards. He called it the 103rd Regimental NCO Club, but he could not deliver on his promises. Regimental Headquarters looked into matters, and first thing we knew, he moved out. Rumors were that he was selling the whiskey for a good markup to the officers. Who knows?*

The officers were getting two bottles per week through the regimental supply system: one bottle of U.S. Three Feathers Blend and one bottle of Australian rum. The Cannon Company officers considered the Australian rum undrinkable. Our amusement ran to taking both bottles to Auckland where we drank the Three Feathers and gave the rum to the band members in the pubs we visited. The results were often hilarious.

Time dims the memory, but the pubs all seemed to be below the sidewalk level of Queen Street in Auckland. In addition, there was some kind of law against having open bottles of alcohol on the tables. Accordingly, the pubs had someone stationed at the top of the steps to shout, "The bobbies are coming," as an alert for us to move the bottles off the table onto the floor.

On one occasion, for reasons that have long escaped me, I was returning to Warkworth from Auckland with only my jeep driver, Pete Hovdenes. We had missed the last ferryboat, so we had to take the long way around the large inlet that separated Auckland and Warkworth. I then suddenly realized that the jeep had a windshield wiper that could be operated only by hand. It wasn't even raining; but the fact that the windshield was right in my face (and I was somewhat inebriated) was enough to inspire a search for an automatic wiper. Pete could not imagine where we might acquire such a thing. But as we passed a bus barn where many of the vehicles were parked awaiting maintenance, I told Pete to stop, and I dashed madly into the barn to "requisition" an automatic wiper for our jeep. In my headlong rush, I fell into a grease pit from which Pete had to extricate me. My uniform was a mess. The effects of the Three Feathers were suddenly dissipated, and my concern was that the men not see me in such a disheveled condition, as it was nearing reveille. I feel sure that the men knew all about it within the hour, but nobody ever spoke of it (to me, at least). Within a week, an automatic windshield wiper miraculously appeared on my jeep.

By this time I was becoming uneasy for news from home. My wife was pregnant when we had left California, and I knew that it was time for our first child to be born. One day I received a telegram that was hopelessly garbled, telling me only "family all well." I assumed this meant the baby had been born, but I had to await a V-mail letter, which arrived several days later, telling me my wife had given birth to a fine, healthy daughter on 3 May 1944. I had arranged with my father-in-law to have one flower delivered to Martha each day for a week. This made me a hero at home, even if I wasn't with Hovdenes, who had witnessed my plunge into the grease pit.

We were generous with three-day passes so that the enlisted men could also go to Auckland. They had fun on these frolics, but their behavior must have been of the highest order, as we never had any incident requiring Military Police intervention or disciplinary action.

Earman: *On a pass, Alfred Gorski and I stayed in Onehunga, south of Auckland, with a Mrs. Frost and her two teenage daughters. We went by tram to His Majesty's Theatre in Auckland accompanied by the girls to see "This Is the Army." A great night! I can remember the girls ordering coffee, and we ordered tea. We went to Ellerslie Racetrack and to an English football game. I also met a nice little New Zealand girl with quite a British accent.*

Leo Machan recalls his three-day pass to Auckland:

Machan: *On three-day passes the troops headed for the beachhead on Queen Street. Sergeant Chester Dilbeck and I went together. We rode the narrow gauge railroad to the city, arriving around 1630 on Saturday afternoon. After we got a hotel room, we went in search of something to eat and drink. We ate "steak and eggs" and had that for every meal. Auckland bars were open from 1100 to 1300 and from 1600 to 1800, resulting in lines outside waiting for the bars to open and six deep inside once they did. The next day we went to a stage show, a musical — "Easter Parade" — and then walked around*

The Cannon Company paraded in Warkworth, New Zealand, on Army Day, 6 April 1944, but alas, Captain Smith was out of step.

the city. I believe the Princess Pat ballroom was open every night except Sunday. There were plenty of girls for dancing. Males were very young or very old, as most New Zealand men had been deployed for the fighting in Europe or elsewhere. We also were invited for dinner in a New Zealand home.

Dinner invitations were typical of the way New Zealand people treated all of us during our stay there.

Army Day was 6 April in the United States, so naturally our regiment staged a parade in Warkworth on that day. A photographer took pictures of each company passing the reviewing stand. The picture of the Cannon Company has become a classic with the Cannoneers: Only I was out of step. My rejoinder has always been that this picture shows everybody in the company out of step except me.

In time, the gun crews got acquainted with the M-7, the officers and fire direction NCOs studied the firing tables and the tactical manuals, and the motor pool and mechanics read the maintenance manuals. The latter was vital to keep our monster weapons on the move. But we needed field exercises to practice the skills we knew only from studying. As a result, we moved south to a training area near the town of Rotorua, a beautiful place near a large lake with a name I never learned to spell and could only make a pass at pronouncing. We had plenty of room to drive the M-7s around and later to fire live ammunition.

Incidentally, while we were in the Rotorua area, we had some cold weather. It even snowed lightly on us. But the men still had their overcoats, thanks to our foresight on New Caledonia. We remarked later that we had trained in the snow for combat that would take place less than 75 miles from the equator.

It was important for our section chiefs and drivers to know the capabilities and limitations of our new vehicles. Accordingly, we drove them up and down slopes that we probably should not have tried. But the M-7s performed beautifully, and the men learned quickly. Since many of our troops had been through field artillery basic training, they already knew a good bit about the 105-mm howitzer.

We knew how to parallel a battery, lay a gun on a designated target, and adjust fire. The principles were the same as with the 75-mm howitzer. But we were uncertain about the kind of missions that might require direct fire at short range on pillboxes — the machine-gun or other heavy weapon nests protected by coconut logs or other revetments — or on other enemy installations. We anticipated the use of "fuse delay" ammunition for this kind of mission, where the shell would explode a fraction of a second after hitting the target. We needed to test that.

We found a wooded area that was perfect for testing. We set up carefully to fire at a large tree at a range of less than 50 yards. To provide for our own

Captain Smith (left) and some of the Cannoneers observe results of test-firing their new weapon, the M-7, at nearly point-blank range. They applied the lessons later in combat.

safety, we used a long lanyard and required all gun crew personnel and observers to position themselves behind the M-7 in order to avoid any flying shell fragments. The first round was a bull's-eye hit on the center of the tree, exploding inside and virtually destroying it. The testing continued, and we found it was safe for the crew to stay in the M-7 for the firing, even at such a short range. The crew was protected from the front by the vehicle's armor.

We gave a lot of thought to the results of this little test, which contributed to the development of tactics we would use many times in combat. But other factors were involved, such as reconnaissance of the target, movement to the firing position, hitting the target with the first round, and rapid evacuation of the firing position. If we failed to destroy the target, we would ourselves become the prime target.

We demonstrated the M-7 for Colonel Cleland and the regimental staff officers. We wanted them to appreciate our capabilities, but we wanted them also to understand that the M-7 was not a tank. It could not fire on the move, and it did not have heavy armor on the sides of the vehicles or a turret that tanks have. It could fire directly on machine-gun nests or other point targets only if we could reconnoiter, show the gunner the target, and move rapidly to a firing position from which we could extricate ourselves immediately after firing. Colonel Cleland was impressed with our capabilities but did not grasp our limitations, as later events would prove.

Long after the war ended, I found in the official history of the 103rd Infantry this glowing reference to our Cannon Company after our arrival in New Zealand:

> The Regimental Cannon Company, just arrived from the States, was used in coordination with the infantrymen of the rifle companies for the first time in these maneuvers. The expertness with which these cannoneers handled their weapons impressed everyone who saw them in action, and the riflemen were glad to have such a powerful ally for the future. The Cannon Company was destined to play a big part in future operations against the enemy.

While we were in the Rotorua area, a few of the men went hunting wild pig with some New Zealand soldiers. They didn't shoot one, but Max Anderson, one of our cooks, "captured" one by covering the garbage pit with litter and grass; the pig fell in. The meat was deemed to be a bit "gamey," doubtless in comparison with the great beef and lamb we were accustomed to eating. If we had captured the pig later in New Guinea, we would have thought it a delicacy.

Near the end of our stay in New Zealand, we gained two additional officers, Lieutenant Howell and Lieutenant Morcom. On one Saturday evening, Lieutenant Howell fell off the rear end of an Auckland tram, severely injuring

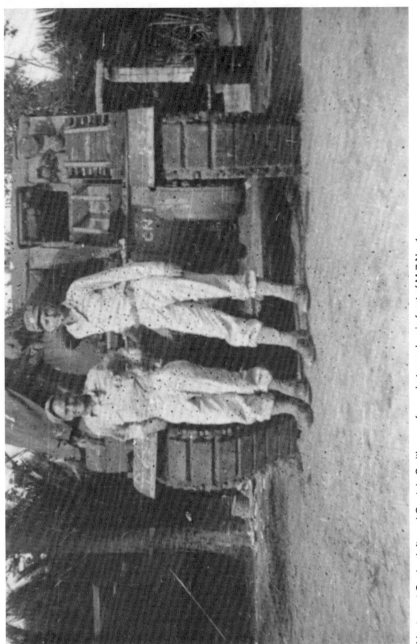

Lieutenant Canjar, left, and Captain Smith pose for a photographer in front of M-7 No. 1.

his head and face. The next morning he came into the mess hall wearing his hat. I informed him that gentlemen remove their hats in the dining room and insisted that he do so. He said that he was ashamed for the men to see his face. But they already knew what had happened, and Lieutenant Howell thereby acquired the permanent nickname "Tram."

In late June, it was time for us to move on. The rumors were that we were going to New Guinea, and the rumors for once were correct. The medics gave shots to all who needed them, causing some men to run a fever for a day or so; however, shots were necessary.

The last incident of note occurred just as we boarded ship. Clarence H. Haug had fallen in love with a Red Cross girl and had requested permission to leave the ship and get married. I objected as strenuously as I had insisted that every member of the company go with us when we deployed from Camp Stoneman. However, his application had to be acted on by the Division Commander, Major General Leonard Wing. I entered into a vigorous conversation with General Wing's aide, but I lost the argument. Permission was granted, and Haug left the ship and got married.

We sailed from Auckland on the USS *Shanks* on 5 July 1944 for Aitape, a village on the north coast of New Guinea. En route, I thought it incongruous that, though we had traveled in blackout conditions all the way across the Pacific, the ship showed a movie on deck while we were passing between New Guinea and the island of New Britain, where the Japanese had a big base at Rabaul. When we arrived, Clarence Haug was already there, having been flown directly from New Zealand.

Chapter 6

New Guinea

Our move to Aitape, about 75 miles west of Wewak, was part of General Douglas MacArthur's strategy of island-hopping. Securing Aitape, which had a major Japanese base, would cut off a large Japanese force from its main support to the west.

There was no natural harbor or docking facility at Aitape, so we demonstrated our ability to climb down the cargo nets into the lighters — craft that helped in the loading and unloading of the ships — to go ashore. This meant that all our supplies would also have to come in that way while we were there.

The 32nd Infantry Division was already fighting the Japanese, who were trying to make their way west, when we arrived at Aitape. The Driniumor River provided a natural barrier, of which the 32nd took maximum advantage. We did likewise when we relieved elements of the 32nd.

As I had anticipated, the jungle came down almost to the beach, and there was no effective way to use the M-7s immediately. Accordingly, we were assigned to a defensive area in the same manner as the rifle companies. We dug foxholes and built bunkers, but our sector was quiet. Our only early casualty was Kenneth Archer, who shot himself in the foot while cleaning a pistol. He was evacuated.

It rained every day, so we needed canvas for the roofs of our bunkers. Leo Machan decided to take care of that.

Machan: *I took several men to the beach where supplies were being landed. While there, a Jap plane flew over the roadstead. There must have been 30 or*

40 ships in the area, and all started firing at the plane. He dropped one bomb, hit nothing, and flew off. Score: Jap 0; U.S. Navy 0. We managed to liberate two tarps. When we got back to the company and unfolded the tarps, they were full of holes and worthless.

A few days later our M-7s arrived by LST (Landing Ship, Tank), but we continued to have rifle-company-type missions in addition to some fire missions with the howitzers.

Having come to the combat zone from the luxury of New Zealand, we were especially conscious of the quality of the food, "mess" being an appropriate term to describe it. At first, we received C rations. That was the Army's oldest form of field rations, usually hash or meat and beans in tin cans, edible only when warmed. These appeared to have been canned years earlier. Soon we graduated to the next level, K rations, which came in small individual boxes wrapped in waxed paper. These were a slight improvement over C rations. Much later in the war we received what was called 10-in-1 rations, so called because ten men could get one meal from a box. This was fine if a squad or gun section was located together and could share a meal. The quality of the food was better than either C or K rations, but some kind of cooking was almost essential. In the course of the war, we ate them all and learned the art of trading around for acceptable meals.

In addition to our rations, we had an unlimited supply of coconuts. The men were fascinated by the great abundance. Using their machetes, they broke them open, drank the milk, and ate some of the meat. But they soon learned the effect of too much coconut milk on the digestive system. Our pit latrines were in danger of filling up.

Speaking of latrines, our urinals consisted of hollow stalks of bamboo stuck into the ground at an angle in various places close to the tents around the company area. They were located conveniently enough to encourage use by almost everyone.

* * * * *

The 103rd Infantry was not encountering many Japanese troops, so the regimental commander decided we should make a "reconnaissance in force" along the coast eastward toward Wewak. He gave that mission to me and assigned a rifle platoon to accompany those of the Cannon Company whom I took on this patrol. I was also afforded the use of a Piper Cub airplane to make a preliminary aerial reconnaissance. However, this was a useless flight, I could not see anything on the ground through the dense jungle. There could have been a regiment of troops there, and I would not have known it. Furthermore, the enemy could have fired at the Piper Cub from their jungle positions and shot us down. I decided that in the future, I would decline the use of the airplane and make my reconnaissance on foot.

For the patrol, I took one Cannon Company platoon with its two M-7s, the rifle platoon, and a small motor maintenance section. We had plenty of firepower and did some firing but never uncovered any organized Japanese unit. The riflemen spotted a single Japanese soldier and shot at him, but he broke all speed records running back into the jungle. We picked up one Japanese straggler to take him back in a trailer, but the doctor said he was too far gone to save; he was suffering, but morphine would kill him. One of the riflemen shot him, alleging that "he tried to escape." Stan Earman said, "I'll never forget it." Leo Machan's comment: "War is hell."

We went about 15 miles along the beach, then returned to Aitape. We had accomplished our mission: We could report that there was no organized Japanese force threatening our positions within 15 miles. Thereafter, we maintained outposts and kept some weapons sited to stop an attack, even if it came from the sea.

On 16 August 1944, the U.S. 6th Army declared the Driniumor River area clear of Japs. We then moved into a semipermanent setup on a "street" with Regimental Headquarters, Service Company, and Antitank Company. Actually, we were at the edge of an old coconut plantation, and we made the most of this. We lived in pyramidal tents, slept on canvas cots (always under mosquito nets), and put up our beautiful Cannon Company, 103rd Infantry, sign we had brought from California. Our mess sergeant and cooks set up the kitchen, and we started getting B rations — large quantities of food that the cooks prepared — which were fine except when the supplies failed to arrive on time. We had "procured" some metal airstrip material that we fashioned into tables, which made for a reasonably satisfactory stand-up dining arrangement, as we had no chairs.

Best of all, we had brought three shower heads, so our men built a shower stand, burned out the inside of three 55-gallon gasoline drums, attached the heads, and mounted them on the stand. By filling the drums in the morning, the water was plenty hot by late afternoon. Antitank Company next door tried to muscle in on our resourcefulness, but soon our NCOs struck a satisfactory deal: The antitank men could use the showers if they would fill the drums every morning.

We were secure in this location and relatively relaxed awaiting our next mission. Poker games were the norm, but they were for low stakes — nickels and dimes. Some of the men had Coleman lanterns for night games, and Ruth Machan sent Leo the necessary accessories for the lanterns.

The officers played under a loose jeep headlight that was connected to the battery of my running vehicle. That sounds like a waste of gasoline, but gas continued to arrive at Aitape in greater quantities than food or anything else,

Lieutenant Rix Maurer (left) and Captain Smith at the Cannon Company command post in Aitape, New Guinea. All were proud of their sign, "Home of the Cannoneers."

so much so it was dangerous. We tried to use as much of it as possible; we even burned the garbage with it. One of the regiments told us that they had to extend their perimeter farther into the jungle to secure an area for the never-ending supply. And all of this while gasoline was rationed at home.

Some of our men went swimming in the surf, trying to ride the waves into shore. It was a new experience for some Midwesterners who got a few scratches from the beach sand. Others played softball or volleyball.

Movies were available every night at a regimental theater with coconut logs for seats. *Tin Pan Alley* with Jack Oakie and Betty Grable was shown so many times that the troops knew the script by heart and spoke the lines along with the actors.

One of our men, Ray Stephens, had a good baritone voice and liked to sing. Warren Evrard had a small ukulele that he played while Stephens, Ken Nelson, and a few others sang. But while we were at Aitape, Stephens was transferred to Special Services at his request. He was a talented musician and a good organizer of entertainment, so this was a logical move.

Some other changes took place for other reasons. One man was busted for making "jungle juice" out of dried peaches from the troop rations. He went to Service Company and later became mess sergeant there. Sergeant Frank Davenport was transferred to Regimental Headquarters S-3 Section; Milo Smisek and Alifonso Abilez went to an infantry rifle company; and L. J. Weis went to Service Company. Lieutenant Ray Moss had always harbored a desire to get back to the field artillery in which he had been commissioned. He got that opportunity in New Guinea, and I did not stand in his way. He had done a fine job for us. Much later, we were all saddened to learn that he had been killed in action. To replace him, we got another field artillery officer, Lieutenant Charles Rice. He also became an important part of our company. We received other replacements as well, including Floyd Hamm and Harry Patterson.

At one point, an unfortunate incident occurred in Sergeant Otto Hof's gun section. Using gasoline to clean the M-7, the men spilled some, and somehow it caught fire. The fire extinguisher put it out but not before William Berwert and Edward Roberts were severely burned. This was in Lieutenant Leo Canjar's platoon, and he reprimanded Leo Machan, the platoon sergeant, for allowing the use of gasoline for this purpose. Many years later I heard from Roberts, who was having difficulty establishing with the Veterans Administration that his injury was service-connected. Leo Canjar, Clint Lee, and I all submitted sworn statements to the VA to substantiate Roberts's claim, but the VA never did tell us the outcome.

The ammunition racks in the M-7s were designed so that the shells stuck up above the side armor plate, thus exposing the fuses, a potentially dangerous setup. Ordnance okayed a modification of the rack so that the shells would lie on their sides instead of standing up. The welder arrived, and then followed an incident Leo Machan remembers:

Machan: *There were "No Smoking" signs stenciled all over the inside of the M-7, but the welder was smoking a cigarette. A higher-ranking officer was going through the area and stopped to see what was going on. He stuck his head over the side and said, "Damn it, soldier, can't you see the 'No Smoking' sign?" The man waved that blazing torch at the officer and said, "What the hell do you think this is?" Very red-faced, the officer said, "Carry on," and snuck off. Then we really exploded with laughter.*

But as a rule, our men respected rank.

Earman: *We stood inspection for General Leonard Wing, and I was thrilled that he talked to me and asked me questions. I was later complimented by our platoon commander on the way I handled myself.*

Occasionally, native boys would come through our area with Japanese souvenirs — helmets, rifles, bayonets, canteens, gun belts, packs, flags. They spoke some kind of garbled language but managed to make themselves understood. They were sharp traders, but Leo Machan tells this story:

Machan: *The only man who ever came out on top was one of our cooks, Max Anderson. He would lure them to the back of the kitchen with food and commence to trade. He had a line of b.s. that wouldn't quit. Then he took out his teeth and laid them down. Then he would grab his ears as though he were removing his head. The natives didn't wait to see what would happen. They took off, leaving their goodies behind and Max laughing with the prizes in hand.*

People who have been in a remote location like Aitape, New Guinea, can understand what it is like to be in a place where it is impossible to buy anything. If you needed toilet articles, cigarettes, or anything that you would normally purchase in a drugstore, in Aitape you had to wait until it was available in the regular rations or through the Special Services Section. Cigarettes, for example, were included in the B rations at one carton per man per week. This was not enough for the heavy smokers, but the nonsmokers shared. Leo Machan found that one of his men was selling his cigarette ration, so he had a short chat with him; he wisely decided he didn't need money that badly. After all, where could he spend it?

One of the most distasteful chores imposed on the officers was censoring all outgoing mail from our men. We had to read — or at least scan — every letter, and they were numerous indeed. But we managed to read them in such a way that we could discover any breach of security without causing us to feel that we were intruding on our men's privacy.

One of our men wrote a letter home that essentially said, "We are now in a new place. I cannot tell you where. I am in my tent looking out at the guineas running around." I called him in and offered to return his letter to him rather than send it forward with a big hole in it. He chose that option after I gave him a rather substantial lecture on security. But throughout our time overseas, we had almost no occasion to use the razor blades we kept in our hands while performing our nightly chore as "censors."

Preparing for the Next Move

Inevitably, the 43rd Division received orders for its next mission. We were to be part of a major amphibious operation to liberate the Philippine island of Luzon, thus fulfilling General MacArthur's promise, "I shall return."

For the Cannon Company, this meant a new challenge, reorganization, some additional weapons, and more responsibility. We were issued five "amphibious tanks," officially designated the LVT-A4 (Landing Vehicle, Tank, model A-4), which were to constitute part of the first wave of the landing force at Lingayen Gulf on the northwest coast of Luzon. We were to get enough additional troops to man these weapons, but, of course, this meant a reorganization so that our experienced men could take the more responsible positions.

The term "amphibious tank" was a piece of overly generous nomenclature. The vehicle slightly resembled a tank in profile but fell short of a tank in significant ways: Its armor plate was far less sturdy than a real tank (it had to be because it was amphibious); its weapon, the 75-mm howitzer, could not be fired with any accuracy while the vehicle was moving; and its crew had less protection and could see less than the normal tank crew. But it was a valuable piece of equipment for this kind of military operation; it enabled the assaulting first wave to have the equivalent of artillery close-support fire immediately available upon hitting the beach. So with the LVT, the Cannon Company had acquired another major weapon system.

These new weapons meant a period of familiarization for the Cannoneers and study of maintenance manuals for the mechanics and motor pool personnel. The process was similar to what we had followed when we had acquired the M-7s in New Zealand, but it was a bit easier because we had already had experience with the 75-mm howitzer in California and the track-laying vehicles in New Zealand and New Guinea.

The major task was reorganization of the company to select capable section chiefs and gun crews. I placed all five LVTs in the second platoon with a combination of experienced and newly appointed section chiefs from among

Captain Smith beside an LVT-A4, one of the amphibious "tanks" that landed with the first wave at Lingayen Gulf, Luzon.

our many capable Cannoneers. This platoon was then able to concentrate its training on its specific amphibious mission while the M-7 crews concentrated on training for the missions they would have when they landed.

The Luzon campaign was to be a major step toward the eventual defeat of the Japanese. With the loss of Manila, the Japanese would be pushed back almost to the defense of their homeland. The 43rd Division was part of an enormous operation; the battle plans were formulated accordingly. We were to land near the town of San Fabian and move rapidly inland. Colonel Cleland, our regimental commander, was determined that every man in the regiment know as much about the future operation as possible.

Anticipating an increased risk of malaria, the doctors doubled our daily dosage of Atabrine. Many did not like to take these tablets, so the regiment issued orders that NCOs or officers would supervise the administration of the medicine.

I prepared a detailed Field Order covering the missions and actions of every element of the Cannon Company in the assault landing and early movement inland. This was approved by Colonel Cleland and published as an annex to the Regimental Operations Order. My Field Order was classified "Top Secret" but was declassified in 1973 and is included in Appendix 2. Several members of the company, in addition to the few in company headquarters, participated in the preparation of this order. For example, Stan Earman and Warren Evrard prepared the many sketch maps and overlays that accompanied it. Those members of the company who have not seen the details of that order will get a chuckle by comparing it with what actually happened.

Using the sketch maps and overlays, I gave detailed briefings to all members of the company, covering terrain where we would land, everything we knew about the enemy dispositions and the planned naval bombardment, and exactly where each element of the Cannon Company would go and what everybody should do. But no military operation ever turns out exactly as planned, and this was no exception.

Our platoon of five LVTs practiced landings every day by going out into deep ocean water, forming up, and moving as rapidly as possible to the beach and assuming firing positions. It was a tough assignment at best. Some of our men did not like the new weapons, nor did they like leaving their old gun sections. But our senior NCOs explained to them the necessity of a mix of experienced personnel with new replacements.

About this time, a certain lieutenant came to me one day asking permission to go to the medical aid station to have the doctor see about some warts on his hand. Of course, I told him to go ahead and get them taken care of before our departure. I never saw him again. The doctors, for some reason, evacuated him to an Army hospital at Lae on the east end of New Guinea. In what seemed only a few days, I received a letter from my wife telling me that this lieutenant was in the hospital at Fort Gordon, had been to our home for dinner with the family, and had enjoyed playing with my new daughter (whom I had never seen). I was incensed for several reasons, including that he had told my wife what tough fighting we had been encountering when, in fact, nothing like that had occurred.

* * * * *

Advance parties are customary for all military operations. In this case, some ships were much faster than others, so elements assigned to the slowest vessels left Aitape first. Two M-7 crews left on 20 December 1944 by LSM (Landing Ship, Medium), a vessel large enough to handle at least two tanks and their associated personnel. But coordination of the naval transports was not as precise, and our advance party wound up in Leyte where Vince Gagliano, George Liebsack, Stan Earman, and others had Christmas dinner. Along with several other ships destined for the Lingayen landing, their LSM finally left Leyte Gulf and joined our convoy. In the meantime, Christmas packages had begun arriving at Aitape, and everyone in the Cannon Company shared with each other.

Loading of the ships proceeded at a slow pace. All our unit equipment, including our tents, was taken away, leaving us with nothing except individual items that we would take aboard ship on our person. Even though we were without tents, we were not allowed to board the ships until the Navy was ready for us. On Christmas Day, the rain came down in torrents. Our individual ponchos proved inadequate. Two men are supposed to be able to button their ponchos together to form a small pup tent, but it just didn't work. Remembering that we still had hundreds of gallons of gasoline, some of our men poured it on a pile of coconut logs, and we had a big bonfire. The Cannon Company assembled around that fire for most of the night singing songs. That was our Christmas celebration.

The next day we boarded our ships and headed for Luzon. We had one unfortunate accident in the boarding process. The seas were a bit high, making it difficult for men with full equipment to get from the small boats to the cargo nets to climb aboard the ships. Sergeant Virgil Dilly did not scramble quite fast enough, and the small boat smashed his foot against the side of the ship, breaking bones in his foot and ankle. He was taken to the hospital and missed the trip. Fortunately, this was our only loading casualty. Maybe that cargo net climbing training at Camp Stoneman had paid off. We would need the same skills to get from the ships to the assault boats going ashore at Lingayen Gulf.

Because of our varied missions, Cannon Company personnel were on three different ships. We bade each other good-bye and good luck, hoping to be reunited on 9 January 1945, which was to be the day we would land on the beaches of Luzon.

En route, some of us witnessed the "kamikaze" attacks wherein Japanese pilots deliberately dove their planes onto our Navy ships. Fortunately, most of them missed their targets. I saw only one plane hit a U.S. ship.

During the trip we also heard Tokyo Rose refer to the 43rd Division as the "Munda Butchers" and say we would receive "a hot welcome to Lingayen from the Imperial Japanese Marines." But this propaganda had no effect on us.

We traveled north through the China Sea, arriving at the Lingayen Gulf on 8 January 1945 for the assault landing the next morning.

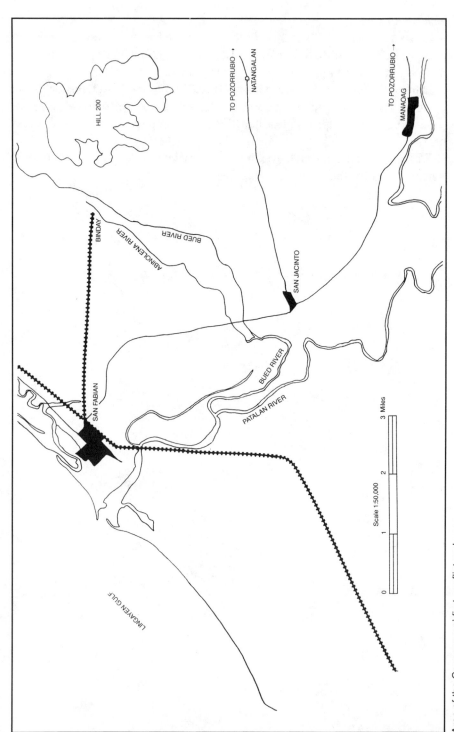

Area of the Cannoneers' first conflict on Luzon.

Chapter 7

Luzon, Philippine Islands

We Go Ashore

A reading of the Cannon Company Field Order for the Luzon landing would reveal that any number of unforeseen conditions or events could disrupt the plan. It is almost always so in a military operation, especially in an amphibious landing on a hostile shore.

The first deviation came when Colonel Cleland directed me to accompany him on his landing craft, which was designated a "free boat"; that is, it was not assigned to a specific wave but could join any when he deemed it advisable to go ashore. I could take one radio operator with me, so I took Warren Evrard.

We expected hostile fire from the beaches, but it did not materialize in our immediate area. This emboldened Colonel Cleland to have his landing craft dart here and there among the other craft lined up in waves, making it readily apparent to anyone on shore that ours was a command boat. I didn't like that idea very much and thought even less of his decision to join the wave that landed eight minutes after the first wave did.

We had no idea what hostile fire awaited us on shore, but I was sure whatever enemy observers were on duty had spotted our boat as a prime target. At that point I instructed Evrard that whichever way the colonel went from the boat, we would go the other way.

Meanwhile, our LVTs had made it ashore safely with the first wave of riflemen, found no organized enemy forces on the beaches, and moved promptly into San Fabian. The first hitch came when they found that the rice paddies were not "hard and dry" as we had been told they would be. The LVTs got bogged down, and the mud made movement difficult and slow for the riflemen.

About this time I encountered the Regimental Executive Officer, Lieutenant Colonel Devine, and asked him, "What's the situation?" His reply: "There ain't no situation; we're just trying to get the troops together." I decided I should do the same thing.

Our M-7s came ashore and moved into an assembly area almost as scheduled. The rifle troops our LVTs were supporting decided to abandon the rice paddies and move toward their objective on the hard-surface road from San Fabian to San Jacinto. This meant trouble for us, as those LVTs had such a high profile and so little armor that they were easy targets for any field guns sited on that road. One LVT was hit, and two of our men were killed, Alvin Isaachsen and Leo Sperdutti. The regimental commander insisted that we continue to use the LVTs as long as possible but soon learned that they were not tanks and could not be used as such in land warfare.

The main body of the Cannon Company spent the first night ashore in a defensive perimeter. A lone enemy soldier infiltrated our position and placed a hand grenade on the track of one of our vehicles, but our gun crew found it in time and no harm was done.

Long Days of Combat Begin

The 103rd Infantry plan was to move rapidly through San Fabian, San Jacinto, and Manaog and take Hill 200, the dominant land feature, by the end of the first day. The Japanese plan was to back its forces away from the beach area during the Navy bombardment, fire on the landing troops with big guns, including 12-inch coast artillery they had presumably taken from Corregidor, then make its main resistance on Hill 200. Thus the battle for the hill was joined.

But taking Hill 200 the first day was far too optimistic for two reasons: It was out of the reach of our naval guns, and the Japanese had dug many caves and placed field guns in them. We took the hill eight days after the landing.

During those eight days of combat, the Cannon Company put into action all the methods of employment we had practiced in New Guinea. The LVTs fulfilled their landing mission and even went beyond the beaches, albeit with some casualties. Our M-7s were in position to provide immediate indirect fire support to the regiment and did so for the advancing riflemen moving toward Manaog and Hill 200.

We soon encountered the need to use the M-7s for direct fire on those enemy field guns located in caves or in coconut-log pillboxes. These actions required a disciplined approach by the officer directing the fire, the section chief, the driver, and the gun crew; all played critical roles. We found that we could destroy those enemy targets in just the way we had practiced. When called upon to execute these missions, all of our gun crews performed in a skillful and courageous manner.

After Hill 200 was taken on 17 January, the action continued through the barrios (villages) of Pao, Dilan, Malasin, Talogtog, Pozorrubio, and Bina-lonan with the regiment taking Hill 600 and then Hill 800. There seemed always to be just one more "commanding hill" that had to be conquered.

We paused at Pozorrubio long enough for the Cannon Company to dig in with a strong perimeter defense. I recall that the company command post was dug in at least six feet. Also, we had "picked up" from various sources enough sound-powered telephones that we had communications with almost every foxhole around our perimeter.

The Japanese had a heavy field gun we called "Pistol Pete" in a firing position from which it could reach us. One day a heavy round landed about 50 yards behind us; a second round came in about the same distance in front of us. We were sure they would split the difference and the next round would land in our perimeter, and it did. Sensing that the round had exploded near the position of Sergeant Leonard Schoneman, I picked up the phone and asked, "Schoneman, can you tell where that one landed?" His immediate answer: "Sir, I think it landed in the shithouse." I could hear laughter all over the company position.

Schoneman was right. Our beautiful latrine had been destroyed, but the enemy failed to follow up with more fire. A detail repaired the damage.

Our worst experience of the war had come on 14 January 1945. The regiment was advancing through a valley on a wide front. Intelligence reports (which we had learned always to doubt) indicated little, if any, organized resistance, so the regimental commander decided that we could move more rapidly with the M-7s alongside (instead of behind) the advancing rifle troops. I should have made a stronger objection to this procedure than I did. After all, the M-7 was not a tank — it couldn't fire while moving, and it was not smart to have it out front. But because the resistance was reported to be so light, I failed to do so. Leo Machan describes the incident vividly:

Machan: *We moved through a valley, very hilly country, in support of infantry but ahead of the troops. We went over the crest of a hill and stopped: A Jap gun was spotted. Sergeant Terracina's M-7 was nearly broadside and had to swing around to fire. As soon as he moved, the M-7 was hit, killing Terracina and Corporal Aveggio, his gunner. The gun crew jumped off the M-7 and went to the rear down the hill. Leroy Kumbier and I were the only men left. Kumbier was bleeding from a gash under his eye, but he said he was okay. The artillery started firing on the gun position, and we left the hill to join the other gun on our right. We met Joe Baker who was hunting the aid station, which I had just passed. I took him there and witnessed our CO get really pissed off at* *the regimental commander and slam his helmet to the ground. Terracina's M-7 was retrieved that evening. The other platoon M-7 was hit in the pulpit. Jesse Adams was killed. I felt bad and didn't sleep very well that night.*

The above is an accurate description. I was incensed because Colonel Cleland had told me that we were later to repeat the maneuver in the same manner that had gotten three of our men killed. Despite my unprofessional behavior, I did prevail in that dispute: Cleland's order was later rescinded. I did not realize until many years later that anyone had seen my tirade against my regimental commander. Leo Machan and Jim Durham, my radio operator, described the scene to me just a few years ago at one of our reunions. Obviously, the men in the company knew more than I thought they did. Leo Machan learned the right lessons from this experience:

Machan: *I think it was a total breakdown in our training discipline. We did everything wrong. First, we were used as tanks. Second, we should have been supporting infantry. Third, we pulled on top of the hill and stopped — sitting ducks. Fourth, when the M-7 had to swing around, the machine gunner did not open up on the target.*

Another incident occurred when I spent the night with one of the battalions. At about 0200, the Japanese launched an attack on one of our rifle companies. We could see the fire fight from the command post. The battalion commander, Lieutenant Colonel Welch, asked me if we could place fire on the attacking enemy. I remembered a target registration we had made before — the men knew how to set their sights on that particular point — and I could see exactly where the Japanese were located. Knowing that the fire would have to be delivered quickly and with precise accuracy, I gave the necessary fire mission data to Lieutenant Clint Lee and cautioned him that each gun crew should be especially careful in leveling the bubbles on the gun sights — we didn't want to hit our own men. I called for two rounds from each gun.

When the first rounds landed, the rifle company commander reported to the battalion commander that our fire was landing on them. Colonel Welch was naturally quite upset. I told him that the men should hunker down because the next salvo was already on the way. The following message from the rifle company commander was that the Japanese attack had been repelled and that our fire had not caused any casualties in his company. In fact, we hadn't hit their company at all, but this was an easy mistake for them to make in the dark with the enemy attacking. We had placed eight 105-mm explosions on that Japanese attack force. That kind of precision fire in the middle of the night under adverse conditions could only come from gun crews who were both highly skilled and conscientious. I was proud of them.

The Cannon Company command post somewhere in Luzon with Captain Smith (in chair), Leo Machan, and Ken Nelson.

On one occasion when I had been with the rifle troops for a good many consecutive days, First Sergeant Kenneth Nelson told me that the men thought I needed a good night's uninterrupted sleep. He had procured a blackout tent, placed a canvas cot in it, and told me I should sleep there overnight. I claimed I did not need it, but I knew he was right, and I had a sound rest.

The next morning one of the men asked me, "What do you want us to do with this Jap?"

"What Jap?" I replied.

"The one we killed outside your tent during the night." I had slept so soundly I didn't even hear the rifle shot. I was thankful that the men had looked after me by arranging for my rest and protecting me in the tent.

* * * * *

In an attack situation — which was most of the time on Luzon — many of our men took turns manning an observation post to control our indirect fire and to communicate with our gun crews. The OP was always placed so that we could see the enemy positions, and if the enemy discovered that we were directing fire from there, they would certainly fire at us. It was hazardous duty. The officers took turns as Forward Observers on the OP. I tried to pull my full share but also had to spend a lot of time with the rifle battalion commander we were supporting so I could advise him on what we could provide. Our company was used constantly.

Stan Earman describes his part in one of our saddest incidents:

Earman: *I was reluctant to go to the OP again after having just come back from it and having dug a beautiful foxhole for the night. I was very tired but had to go nevertheless. We called for fire, and one of our 105s had a muzzle burst. I never did find out how many were injured or lost. I was told how fortunate I was to be on the OP that night because my foxhole caught lots of shrapnel and I would have been killed. I still have several pieces of this shrapnel.*

The muzzle burst was on Sergeant William Kopy's gun. Leo Machan described it this way:

Machan: *Fire mission last evening. Kopy's gun firing mostly harrassing fire. Kopy standing on rear deck of the M-7. I was on the phone behind the vehicle relaying fire commands to him. Gun fired; muzzle burst. Kopy hit bad; belly full of holes. Other men also hit but Kopy evacuated that night. Other men treated at hospital in morning.*

Defective ammunition must have caused the accident. It was the only such incident that happened to us.

After the first 38 days of combat, the regiment had suffered 172 killed in action, 1 missing in action, and 551 wounded in action. But enemy casualties had been higher than ours by a ratio of 10 to 1. The Cannon Company took a few brief days to get replacements, then moved about 40 miles south to Guimba, then another 40 miles south to the Clark Field area. After a few days but little action there, we moved another 60 miles south and bivouacked on the lawn of the Wack Wack Country Club near Manila.

Not much time had elapsed since our last combat situation. We launched our next attack, attached to the 1st Cavalry Division, from the country club lawn on 9 April. The S-2 briefing told us we were facing 6,000 well-organized enemy troops. Frequently in combat, our platoons were placed in two or three different locations, not only to provide support to more than one rifle battalion but also to avoid having the company wiped out by one artillery barrage. This advance continued for many days, and we had plenty of occasions to use the M-7 in direct fire on enemy pillboxes in caves. Our forces then took the town of Antipolo.

The Cannon Company continued to be used for both indirect fire support and direct fire on pillboxes in this and the next campaign beginning on 7 May along Laguna de Bay southeast of Manila through the barrios of Pangil, Siniloan, Mabitac, and Santa Maria. These were sad sights, as the villages had been virtually destroyed by the retreating Japanese and our heavy fire.

Before our last major campaign — to capture intact the Ipo Dam, which supplied water for the city of Manila — we were pleased to welcome back to the company Sergeant Virgil Dilly, our supply sergeant, whose foot had been broken while climbing the landing nets at Aitape. This campaign action continued until nearly the end of June.

Constant patrolling was also the order of the day for as long as we were on Luzon, as pockets of resistance continued. Many individual Japanese soldiers did not surrender; some stayed in caves or were otherwise hidden for several years after the war ended.

That the Cannon Company was kept busy is evident in some of my notebook records of ammunition consumption. For example, for preparatory fire followed by five days of action beginning 8 April and the first six days beginning 7 May, our daily consumption of high explosive and smoke rounds was as follows:

8 April — 53 HE, 3 smoke	7 May — 7 HE, 2 smoke
9 April — 24 HE	8 May — 197 HE, 9 smoke
10 April — None	9 May — 64 HE
11 April — 17 HE, 5 smoke	10 May — 175 HE, 18 smoke
12 April — 101 HE, 5 smoke	11 May — 202 HE, 19 smoke
13 April — 104 HE, 8 smoke	12 May — 95 HE, 8 smoke

The Cannon Company in bivouac during combat in Luzon.

In late May and through most of June the ammunition consumption continued at this general rate. When we engaged targets pointed out to us by the rifle troops, we used smoke rounds to adjust our fire. We did not need smoke rounds when we fired on pillboxes by direct, point-blank fire.

When we used harrassing fire, it was usually on crossroads or other locations that we anticipated enemy troops would utilize if they made any movements at night or on suspected bivouac areas to keep the enemy from sleeping. All such rounds were preplanned and fired at irregular intervals to keep the enemy from anticipating the next round.

Our gun crews worked out a system to prevent harrassing fire duty from keeping all of them awake at night: After the gun was laid on its target, one gun crew member could fire the rounds by himself while the rest of the troops slept.

One day when I was at our gun positions, one of the gun crews came to me and said that they had all the fun getting to do so much firing and that I never had the opportunity for enjoyment like that. So they decided to make me a temporary member of the gun crew so that I could have some fun firing our weapons. I was proud to do it and pulled the lanyard on several fire missions.

* * * * *

We continued to receive occasional replacements for men who had been lost to us. Late one afternoon, the first sergeant told me that one of our replacements had claimed he could not stay with us because he was a "psycho case" and that he was not an infantryman but with the military police. I told the first sergeant to have Don Campbell, the company clerk, check the man's service record as soon as possible, but, in the meantime, he would have to spend the night in a foxhole. I think he shared the hole with Sergeant Leonard Schoneman, who must surely have stayed awake all night. The next day Campbell told us the man was indeed what he claimed, so we sent him back for reassignment. This was typical of the difficulties of the personnel system in trying to supply the needed manpower in the Pacific when the war in Europe was still going on.

Our Table of Organization called for a company strength of 102. We landed on Luzon with about 125 because of the added platoon of LVTs. But at times our company strength dropped well below the number required to fulfill all our missions. A notebook in which I jotted down items of concern shows that we dropped to 79 present for duty on one occasion and to 73 on another.

Occasionally, men in combat have urgent needs for supplies to keep the ground fighting going on. I listed some typical items in my notebook:

— 3rd Platoon needs a drum of gas, a pail of bogie grease, and

Captain Smith and his driver, Harold "Pete" Hovdenes, during a lull in fighting at Paete, Luzon.

Berwert's pistol.
— 2nd Platoon needs 2 drums of gas, 10 gallons of oil, 2 reels of
130 wire, grease for the M-7s, and cigarettes.
— 1st Platoon needs more maps and protractors, halazone, and 5 .
bandoliers of M-1 rifle ammunition.
— Lt. Canjar needs a map board, Lt. Maurer needs a field bag,
Sheets needs his helmet, and all platoons want their mail.

Despite almost constant combat, there were a few diversions. First Sergeant
Ken Nelson acquired a little monkey. Leo Machan described the animal's
exploits this way:

Machan: *Damn pest. Pisses all over everything. Floyd Hamm was working
on a jeep motor when the little ape jumped up and spilled a bunch of parts.
Hamm threw a wrench at the monkey. It bounced off a truck and hit Max
Anderson in the back of his head; knocked him pretty silly for a few seconds.*

Another diversion was cock fighting:

Machan: *Cock fighting was a great sport here. Lots of money won and lost
on these fights. Third platoon acquired a white cock who won several fights
and was matched against a cock owned by a couple of Filipinos. The platoon
pooled their money, bet on the white cock, and lost it all.*

About this time Lieutenant Charles Rice, our field artillery officer, asked
for the opportunity to return to his basic branch in our division artillery, which
had openings. I could not object; but we then needed another officer. I
concluded that a battlefield direct commission for Ken Nelson, our first
sergeant, was the ideal solution to the problem. He had all the professional
qualifications to be an officer; he knew our weapons and tactics; and the men
trusted and respected him. I made all these points with the regimental
commander and also pointed out that any replacement infantry officer would
be unlikely to understand our methods of employing our weapons. He
concurred, and Ken Nelson was commissioned a second lieutenant.

That meant an opportunity to promote a new first sergeant. I immediately
selected Leo Machan. For a few days we had an infantry first sergeant transferred into the Cannon Company, but I objected and managed to get him
transferred out and Leo promoted. He was then sent to the nearby 43rd
Division First Sergeants School for a few weeks.

The men had names for all the officers. Nelson was "First Shirt" when he
was first sergeant, but his name was changed to "Baldy" when he became a
lieutenant. I was always "The Old Man." Lieutenant Lee was "Bluebeard,"

and Lieutenant Canjar was called "Preacher." Other men had such names as Blue Baron, Sam the Man, Aveege, Ike, and Zoot.

The M-7s had names as well. I remember the Clarabelle, Milliebelle, Jezebel, Ourbelle, Lulabelle, and Mia Amigo, but their identifications by platoon have escaped me in the passage of time.

* * * * *

About the first of July, the division was relieved of its combat mission, and we moved to Camp LeCroix near Cabanatuan, 50 or 60 miles north of Manila. The Cannon Company was given the mission of laying out and lining up the tents in perfect rows. I presumed this was because we had more aiming circles — sophisticated compasses — than any other unit in the regiment.

On 16 July 1945 my service with the Cannon Company came to an end. Lieutenant Colonel Ray Kinch, commander of the 2nd Battalion, 103rd Infantry, had asked for me to become his Battalion S-3, and the regimental commander approved. I really did not want to leave the Cannon Company, but I had no choice in the matter. Therefore, I chose to look on the bright side. If I ever expected to get promoted, I would have to move to higher headquarters assignments, and Battalion S-3 was a normal step toward promotion to major. Colonel Kinch was a fine battalion commander, and my time with him was a good experience.

The 2nd Battalion was mainly engaged in patrolling. We had several thousand Philippine guerrillas attached to us, so I had the responsibility of organizing a large force for combat operations. However, the Cannon Company was constantly on my mind.

When the regimental commander told me I would be going to 2nd Battalion, I recommended Lieutenant Clint Lee to succeed me as Cannon Company commander. Colonel Cleland readily approved, and Lieutenant Lee took over the company on 17 July. Leo Machan returned from First Sergeants School, reporting that he had not learned a great deal but knew that "VD is carried as LD on MR." Translation: "Venereal disease is carried as line of duty on the morning report."

Mail began flowing with improved regularity. This enhanced the reputation of Bernard J. Bruha, the Cannon Company mail clerk who had often been berated by the troops when he failed to bring mail. He was also the company barber but did not receive particularly high praise for that work either. He had two thankless jobs.

Soon after his promotion to first sergeant, Leo Machan was hospitalized at the 21st Field Hospital. He passed a kidney stone and commented that "now I have an inkling of what childbirth must be like." He was back to duty in six days.

Most of the troops, including those in Cannon Company, were getting a well-deserved rest at Camp LeCroix. Payday was described as "pretty wild," but no Cannoneers went AWOL. Stan Earman describes activities at this time:

Earman: *We saw the popular musical "Oklahoma" while there and a football game in Rizal Stadium in Manila. In a regimental military ceremony I was awarded the Bronze Star medal by Colonel Joseph P. Cleland, along with several other men of our Cannon Company.*

I had recommended many of our men for medals, not all of which were approved. I thought that every member of the Cannon Company, 103rd Infantry, was a hero and still do.

The division was awaiting word of its next move, with almost everyone anticipating that it would be to the homeland of Japan. The rumors were correct.

We Plan Operations in Japan

Colonel Joseph Cleland, the 103rd Infantry commander, was selected for promotion to brigadier general, and Colonel N. G. Bassitt became the regimental commander. When he received the 103rd Infantry mission for the landing on the island of Honshu, he pulled me from the 2nd Battalion and gave me the assignment to organize the loading of all personnel and equipment on the ships assigned to us in accord with our combat operation plan. He called the job "Regimental Transport Quartermaster," a term that I do not think described it very well. That gave me another connection with the Cannon Company, as the loading, transport, and unloading of the company and its M-7s would be important to the assault landing.

I worked on my assignment at Subic Bay Naval Base, near Manila, where I had access to Navy officers who would be working with me and to the detailed information about each ship we would be using. I had little cardboard templates of every truck, M-7, antitank gun, and piece of equipment the regiment would take to Japan and arranged them on scaled drawings of the loading space of our ships to determine in what order they would come off.

While I was engaged in this process and the Cannon Company was formulating its detailed plans, the Japanese surrendered. Colonel Bassitt told me to stick to my task, as we would be going to Japan "combat-loaded" just as we would have if there had been no surrender. This was a prudent step, as no one could be certain of the behavior of the Japanese when we arrived. We would be part of the first occupation troops. If all went well, we were to dock at Yokohama and proceed to Tokyo. That was the way it turned out.

Lieutenant Clinton Lee, Cannon Company commander, remembers the loading this way:

Devastation left by retreating Japanese troops in Paete, Luzon.

Lee: *We were ordered to break camp, load up all equipment and vehicles and men, and head for the docks in Manila. We spent the entire day and evening loading ship. When we woke up the next morning, the ship was pulling away from the dock. I looked down and there were two of the company's M-7s still on the dock. I had signed for them on the books. I wonder what became of them?*

If anyone had ever asked who was responsible, the answer would have been Lieutenant Lee or me. He had signed for them, but I was responsible for the loading of all equipment of the regiment.

Chapter 8

Japan

We Arrive in Japan

Part of the Cannon Company sailed from Manila on 31 August 1945 aboard the USS *Dade*, one of many old ships transporting troops around the Pacific area, and arrived at Yokohama on 2 September, where some elements of the division had already landed. (The company was always divided for movement, since we supported different elements of the regiment.) The mission of the 43rd Division in Japan was to begin the occupation. This was to be accomplished in steadily expanding concentric circles outward from the Tokyo-Yokohama area, principally using the battalions as the occupying forces. Having completed my assignment at Regimental Headquarters, I returned to my job as S-3 of the 2nd Battalion and became involved in this occupation process.

The Cannon Company did not have a major assignment in the occupation but was available, along with the Antitank Company, for any mission the regimental commander might assign.

Leo Machan remembers the arrival in Japan this way:

Machan: *I was much surprised. All the bombing we had done over there had resulted in little damage to the docks. We slid into a dock and marched off down the gangplank. The Japanese were operating the big gantry cranes unloading our ships. After falling into formation and marching back and forth along the dock, we finally boarded trucks. We passed through block after block of burned areas that were once homes. These firestorms must have been terrible.*

Like Machan, I was struck by the lack of damage to the docks, which I would have expected to be prime targets. The rest of Tokyo was devastated except for the emperor's palace, which was standing virtually undamaged.

Stan Earman was aboard a ship that landed at Yokohama on 13 September. He describes Cannon Company experience in Japan this way:

Earman: *We spent the first night in a dockside warehouse. Jim Durham and I were to go again on advance detail to prepare camp at Matsugahara airfield near Kumagaya. While waiting for the Japanese train to depart, we went souvenir hunting and traded candy and cigarettes for a kimono and other silk articles. Then we walked into a movie theater and were enjoying a Japanese film when an MP asked us to leave because an American had been stabbed there the day prior. In the meantime, our train had departed and our equipment with it. We caught a ride in a jeep and got there after the train. We located some of our equipment. We erected tents, but during the night a hurricane-type wind blew our tent down along with others. One of the men had his Army cot tied to the tent flap, and he went for a ride on his cot.*

Ready to Go Home

The Cannon Company received no mission in the occupation because word soon came that the 43rd Division would be relieved by a division en route from Europe. All men in the 43rd Division who had enough points to qualify would be going home. The point system was based principally on time in service, time overseas, and time in combat. This meant that the original members of the Cannon Company would go home. Replacements who had not been overseas long enough were transferred to the 1st Cavalry Division, which would be staying a while.

Machan: *There was a scramble for war souvenirs. We were allowed to take either a sword, rifle, or pistol. I had a sword but wanted a pistol and couldn't trade. I called our old CO but he couldn't help me. Finally, Nelson traded with me, so I have a Nambu 7-mm pistol.*

Stan Earman acquired a Japanese rifle and something else of greater importance:

Earman: *A Japanese notebook that I brought with me from a cave on Luzon came in handy to copy down the names and addresses of 81 of my buddies. From 1986 to the present it has been quite valuable in helping to locate these men again.*

Most of the members of the Cannon Company boarded the USS *General*

Hershey on 27 September and sailed for home on 30 September. Lieutenant Clint Lee was the commander of Army troops on this ship for the trip home.

Chapter 9

Return to the USA

The USS *General Hershey,* carrying 62 original members of the Cannon Company, other soldiers transferred into the company for transportation purposes, and troops from other units who had enough points to go home, sailed from Yokohama to San Francisco despite rumors that it was going to Seattle. Another unfounded rumor was that departure would be delayed until General Leonard Wing's ship could leave so that he would be the first to land in the USA.

With the war over, soldiers had little on their minds except getting home. The Navy found it difficult to impose discipline on the troops, especially when they were asked to perform unpleasant shipboard duties. I was not on the same ship with the Cannon Company; I returned on the USS *Kenton.* Leo Machan describes that trip on the *General Hershey:*

Machan: *We had the usual lifeboat drills and battle stations. The Navy wanted the ship to look good, so troops were put to work chipping paint. But too many hammers were dropped overboard, so that detail was called off.*

The Cannon Company had to furnish a detail to break out ship stores of food items and the like, so Sergeant Hof was put in charge of 15 men for that job. The men were given a button to wear that read "Ship Detail" and were allowed to go to the head of the chow line. Troops were fed in two long lines, which made for a long wait to eat. Hof gave me a button, and I bucked the chow line also. Several days out I went to the head of the line, and an MP turned me back. There must have been a hundred men all wearing a "Ship Detail" button. I smelled a rat and did some checking. It seems that while the detail had been working in the hold, they had found a whole box of buttons and were selling them for a dollar apiece. I wondered which one of the troops had thought up that idea, but no one squealed, and I never found out.

One evening I was trying to find a shortcut but got lost below decks and couldn't find my way topside. Wandering down one hallway, I saw an open door; sailors were eating inside. I stuck my head in to ask for directions when someone invited me to sit down, so I did. I think he was a Philippine waiter. He gave me a menu, and I ordered. There was only one meat dish offered, but I ate my meal and talked with the sailors. I found out that I was in the Chiefs' Mess. I asked if I could eat there every day, so the waiter called the Mess Chief who said if I had 30 cents a meal, I could eat there ten times a day. You couldn't beat that, so I ate there for the rest of the voyage.

When we boarded the ship, we were supposed to turn in our Japanese weapons to be stored for safety reasons. I told our troops to hide theirs because they probably wouldn't get them back, so they hid rifles and swords in mattresses. Just as I had predicted, the sailors and officers took the best weapons.

We had to listen to a chaplain who lectured us on how to behave when we landed in the States. He told us to act like gentlemen and not wild beasts. He must have thought we were savages of some sort.

We sailed into the docks of San Francisco the morning of 10 October 1945. A band was on the dock along with banners reading "Welcome Home." The ship carrying General Wing was already docked. When he marched off, a few speeches were made, and we got off. USO girls and the Red Cross had cold coffee and doughnuts.

From there, it was on to Camp Stoneman and processing. We turned in our equipment, and men started leaving for separation centers near their homes. The property book had to be cleared and the final Morning Report submitted. Lieutenant Lee, Corporal Sinerchio, and I were the last to leave. I took one more souvenir home — our Cannon Company guidon.

Chapter 10

The Second Coming Together

From Camp Stoneman, California, members of the Cannon Company dispersed to their homes all over the United States and picked up their normal lives. After their years as soldiers, they resumed their work as farmers, businessmen, bankers, mechanics, and all the other usual American careers. Almost everybody saved mementos of their war experiences to remind them of the camaraderie that had been theirs in the Cannon Company, 103rd Infantry. The Army then stopped using cannon companies after the first reorganization of the military following World War II.

As these men pursued their civilian lives, there were few chances for members to see each other. But when those opportunities did arise, men made short visits while on business travel or had telephone contact.

Sometime in the 1960s, Clint Lee and I, with our wives, attended a national reunion of the 43rd Infantry Division in Newport, Rhode Island. No other members of our Cannon Company were there, nor could anyone give us leads toward locating any of our fellow Cannoneers. We had effectively lost contact with the men who had meant so much to us in the past.

The years passed and retirement time came for most of us. Clint Lee and his wife, Verda, moved to Vero Beach, Florida, about 50 miles south of Martha and me in Satellite Beach, so we were able to get together often.

With so many retired veterans moving to Florida, a Sunbelt Chapter of the 43rd Infantry Division Veterans Association was holding annual reunions in Orlando. We and the Lees attended those meetings regularly and enjoyed seeing old friends of the division but never saw any other members of our Cannon Company.

Stan "Shorty" Earman, whose memories helped produce this book and whose newsletters help keep our group together now.

Our break came in April 1985 when both Clint Lee and I saw the name of Leo J. Machan, with an address, in a military publication. He had joined the 103rd Infantry Veterans Association in which Clint and I also held membership. I wrote immediately to re-establish contact with Leo, giving him a brief recap of my career.

His reply brought the first real news of our buddies of the Cannon Company. He reported the postwar deaths of Joe Rejsak, Leonard Schoneman, Art Aspegren, and Fred Gustafson. But he had been in contact at various times with Rix Maurer, Leo Canjar, Freddie Bartholomew, Barney Bruha, Don Campbell, Ed Juresic, Ted Jackson, Mike Sinerchio, Chester Dilbeck, Virgil Dilly, and Ken Nelson.

The Machans and the Dillys joined us at the 43rd Infantry Division reunion in January 1986, and the process of re-assembling the Cannon Company was underway with letter writing and telephone calling. For the January 1987 reunion, Ken Nelson, Harold "Pete" Hovdenes, and Don Campbell and their wives joined the Lees, Machans, and Smiths. The guidon Leo Machan had saved from the end of the war became our rallying point and Cannon Company "Command Post" beside the hotel swimming pool. About 25 units of the division had procured new guidons like those they had carried in the war, but ours was the only original displayed and used in the annual tribute to fallen comrades. It was a star feature as other veterans came to touch and admire it.

The number of our Cannoneers attending these Florida reunions increased each year. In 1989 there were nine — Clint Lee, Leo Machan, Don Campbell, Stan Earman, Bud Cochran, Jim Durham, George Liebsack, Vince Gagliano, and me — most with wives.

When Stan Earman arrived, the future growth of our re-assembling Cannon Company was assured. He became the driving force of our reunions. He started an intra-company newsletter that he titled *Fire Mission!* to provide news about members and to encourage attendance at the reunions every January in Orlando.

His chatty newsletter helped bring back old memories. For example, his first *Fire Mission!* asked who remembered names of the "theater in Paso Robles, the store in Jolon and the two bars across the street from each other in Paso Robles." In the next newsletter, he gave the answers — the Hi Ho Theater, Duck's Store, and Lyle's and Johnny's bars. That kind of clever writing helped keep everyone interested.

Stan and Mary Earman have driven many thousands of miles to visit and locate Cannon Company members. On one trip alone in 1989, they went on a 15-day, 4,034-mile, 14-state "buddy finding" mission. The difficulty of locating current addresses after more than 40 years is illustrated by the Earmans' experience on a trip to California where they found a big collection of telephone books in a library. After several afternoons spent poring over those books, Stan came up with leads for finding 19 of our men. In his next newsletter he reported that "through making many, many calls I have so far found three of our buddies."

His *Fire Mission!* newsletters continued to stimulate interest in locating other members and in attendance at the reunions. George Liebsack located Bud Cochran, Lawson Bleich, Carl Schomerus, and Milo Smisek. Vince Gagliano located Louis Beinlich and John DePue. Later, Guy Epperson and his wife, Doris, located Kenneth Archer, Dean Cook, David Kennedy, Clarence Waldhier, Chester Dilbeck, Julio Acosta, and Jack Ratliff.

In the course of all this "buddy finding" activity, several mini-reunions resulted. In early 1990, Stan Earman, Don Campbell, and Harry Patterson called on Frank Chea, a former cook, who treated our reunion to a memorable luncheon. Also, in the summer of that year, George Liebsack organized a small gathering with Milo Smisek, Carl Schomerus, Joe Chadwell, and Leo Machan. This is now referred to as the "annual western reunion" of the Cannon Company because it is alternately held in Iowa and Nebraska, far west of Florida. The August 1991 "western reunion" drew the attendance of Bud Cochran, Guy Epperson, George Liebsack, and Leo Machan at Milo Smisek's home in Wilbur, Nebraska, where they were treated to a feast.

The roster grew to 37 members by the end of 1989, to 41 by the end of 1990, and passed 50 before the end of 1991, despite the occasional death of a member.

The 1991 reunion of the 43rd Infantry Division attracted 15 Cannon Company members, the largest of any company-size unit of the division. In attendance were Jim Durham, George Liebsack, Bob Cannady, Clint Lee, Leo Machan, Don Campbell, Ken Nelson, Jerry Bernas, Stan Earman, J. W. Buchanan, Joe Chadwell, John DePue, Vince Gagliano, Guy Epperson, and I.

An important element of these reunions is the participation of the wives. Without exception they have joined enthusiastically in the social activities and have listened intently to accounts of wartime experiences of their husbands, including many stories in this history.

Most of the members were not married while the troops were overseas, but the wives of those who were maintained a communications network to exchange information derived from letters. This was especially true during some long periods when it was almost impossible for the men to write home. My wife, Martha, recalls that often days, maybe weeks, passed with no letters. Then one day the postman would bring six or eight at the same time. She then passed along snippets to parents of the other officers. Other wives did the same. Martha Smith said that "none of us ever met in person, but it seemed as if we were family." Wives who joined the "family" after the war are now essential to its continued success.

At every gathering of these veterans, a special tribute is paid to those

Nineteen members of the Cannon Company attended the 1992 43rd Infantry Division reunion. Seated (l. to r.): Stan Earman, Clint Lee, W. Stanford Smith, Ken Nelson, and Leo Machan. Second row: Bob Cannady, J. W. Buchanan, George Liebsack, Curtis Banker, Jim Durham, and John DePue. Back row: Don Campbell, David Kennedy, Guy Epperson, Joe Chadwell, Milo Smisek, Vince Gagliano, and Lee Schmidt. Frank Chea was not in the picture.

members who gave their lives in service to their country and to those who have died since the end of World War II. As long as any members of the Cannon Company, 103rd Infantry, remain alive, this special camaraderie will continue to flourish. Perhaps Leo Machan put it best when he wrote that "the pleasures of old friendships become more precious as the years fly by."

The roster that follows in Appendix 5 is an ever-changing honor roll.

Epilogue

New Zealand Revisited

In December 1991 my wife and I visited New Zealand, traveling as passengers on a British containership. One of our purposes was to visit the community where the Cannon Company had been billeted in 1944 and to locate our specific area, if possible. We were received with gracious hospitality and more than accomplished our mission.

Until we received a message while on board the freighter, we did not know that the people of New Zealand were planning a 50th anniversary commemoration in 1992 of the arrival of American troops in their country. The chairman of that enterprise, Operation U.S. Down-Under, was David G. Conway, QSM, who described it as a people-to-people program "in which the people of New Zealand are expressing their thanks to the people of the USA for the way in which they defended our land and its inhabitants against aggression and invasion 50 years ago."

David Conway and his wife, Del Sutton, escorted Martha and me to Warkworth. The first thing we learned was that a harbor bridge now makes it unnecessary to take the Devonport ferry to get there. If that had been in existence in 1944, I never would have fallen into the grease pit!

In Warkworth we met Harry Bioletti, author of *The Yanks Are Coming,* a nonfiction book about the experiences of the Americans and the New Zealand people while the U.S. troops were in the country. He had made a thorough study and knew where every unit had been billeted. With his help, I located the specific area within the Rodney Fair Grounds where the Cannon Company had

In 1991, Major General Smith found a hut in Warkworth, New Zealand, just like the one in which he lived in 1944.

The exact
spot where
Captain
Smith was
out of step
leading the
Cannon
Company in
a parade in
Warkworth
on 6 April
1944.

been billeted. The area has now been taken over by sheep.

We also visited the house that had been our division commander's headquarters in Warkworth. It is a beautiful home that carries the name Riverina, now owned by Mrs. Beverley Simmons, who lives there. She had been alerted to our visit and laid out many mementos in the room that had been General Leonard Wing's office.

Back in the business district of Warkworth, we had no difficulty locating the exact place where the Cannon Company had been standing when the parade picture was taken on 6 April 1944 with me out of step. The *Rodney Times,* a local weekly newspaper, interviewed me and took a picture of me standing at the same spot I had been standing when the earlier photo had been taken. The paper ran a story with both pictures and the headline "Out of Step American Commander Revisits 1944 Camp Town."

Martha picked up souvenirs in a Warkworth shop, including enough to provide table favors for all attending the Cannon Company reunion in Orlando in January 1992.

Before leaving the area, we visited the Puhoi Pub, which I remembered as a favorite place to get a local beer. The bartender had been there for 30 years, which was not nearly long enough to remember me. But there were cordial greetings all around, including a free second beer for me when they found I had been a service member in Warkworth.

Operation U.S. Down-Under is planning another commemorative program in 1994 to take note of the 50th anniversary of the second wave of American troops to visit New Zealand, including the 43rd Division and our Cannon Company. We hope to go back for that occasion.

Author's Notes

As I indicated in the text, this work would have been impossible without the assistance and written contributions of Leo J. Machan and Stanley E. Earman. Both retrieved notes they had made during the war, searched their memories, and supplied much of the information lost to my recollection in the intervening years.

Leo J. Machan went back to work for the U.S. Post Office after the war but hated to be inside. When the Korean War broke out, he volunteered for active duty and was sent overseas. After the Korean War, he reenlisted and had tours of duty in Germany, Korea again, Laos, Thailand, and Vietnam. Most of his assignments were in high military headquarters, the G-2/G-3 (Intelligence and Operations) Sections at corps or group level. Between his foreign service tours, he was stationed at Fort Dix, New Jersey; Lafayette, Indiana; Boston, Massachusetts; Madison, Wisconsin; and Fort Sam Houston, Texas, where he retired 1 May 1974 after 32 years, 7 months of active duty. Married nearly 50 years, he and his wife, Ruth, have two daughters. After all of that service, he reports that I was his commanding officer longer than any other officer in his career.

Stanley E. Earman, like many others who served in the Pacific, had malaria for many months after the war. After hospitalization, he went back to work at Hotel Hershey in his hometown of Hershey, Pennsylvania. After two years he went to Thompson College in Harrisburg, Pennsylvania, then worked for the U.S. Department of Commerce for two years, Goodyear Tire & Rubber Company for ten and a half years in various locations, and finally for Air

Products and Chemicals as an office manager for 26 years. He retired in February 1987. He married his wife, Mary, in 1947. They have two daughters. Today his principal hobby is maintaining contact with members of the Cannon Company.

After World War II, I remained in the U.S. Army Reserve while pursuing a newspaper career as a reporter, editor, and association manager. I retired as president of the American Newspaper Publishers Association in 1974. During my newspaper career I held many assignments in the Army Reserve, including one mission to Vietnam and two assignments on the Army Staff in the Pentagon. I returned to extended active duty in January 1975 in the Office of the Secretary of Defense and retired in April 1979 with the rank of major general. Members of the Cannon Company still call me "Captain" or Stan or Smitty, all of which please me.

Appendix 1

Artillery in the Infantry: The Cannon Companies

Unique in U.S. Army history, the cannon companies of World War II provided the infantry regimental commanders direct command of artillery fire support. Except for this wartime experience, the Army organization structures called for all artillery to remain under division or higher command control with the regimental commander required to request fire support even if the artillery was placed in "direct support" of the regiment. Under normal circumstances, requested fire support was provided, but occasions could — and did — arise when it was not because of higher priorities or even ammunition shortages. In these cases, the cannon company could fill the gap.

The Cannon Company in this narrative was armed with six self-propelled 105-millimeter howitzers mounted on tank chassis, which also included ring-mount .50-caliber machine guns. Identified as the M-7, this was the same weapon used by the organic light artillery battalions of the World War II armored divisions. It fired the same ammunition and had essentially the same ranges as the 105-mm towed guns of the infantry division light artillery battalions.

With six M-7s, the Cannon Company had 50 percent more firepower than an artillery battery armed with four towed 105-mm howitzers. This provided the flexibility that enabled the Cannon Company to fire typical artillery missions with four guns while keeping two guns available for direct fire missions on pillboxes and other point targets. Because of this flexibility and dual capability, the Cannon Company of the 103rd Infantry often was attached to one of the regiment's rifle battalions, especially when the battalions were operating far apart.

Because of the similarity of their mission and capabilities, our Cannon Company and the supporting artillery battalion maintained a close relationship. The 152nd Field Artillery Battalion normally provided direct support to the 103rd Infantry Regiment. The artillery battalion commander gave radios to the Cannon Company to ensure direct communications at all times, including an artillery radio in the Cannon Company commander's jeep. The artillery radios were much more reliable over greater distances than the organic infantry radios.

The Cannon Company gun position was always plotted on maps in the artillery battalion Fire Direction Center, and direct communication was always maintained by wire or radio or both. In this fashion, the Cannon Company weapons were available to accept fire missions from the field artillery battalion when the artillery had more missions than it could accept and the Cannon Company gun position was within range of the requested target, assuming, of course, that the company was not already engaging another target and that it had sufficient ammunition. This system worked well throughout the long Luzon campaign.

Members of the Cannon Company gun crews had trained in standard artillery methods of accepting and executing fire missions. Cannon Company officers had received specialized training at Fort Benning, Georgia, including standard artillery methods of observing and directing fire as well as issuing fire commands to gun crews. The original cadre for the Cannon Company, 103rd Infantry, came from the field artillery, and most of the gun crew members received their basic training in the field artillery. For these reasons, close integration with the supporting artillery battalion was relatively easy for both the Cannon Company and the artillery Fire Direction Center.

To establish a basis for accepting fire missions in a target area, it was necessary to establish a base point within the target area — usually a prominent land feature, easy for the Forward Observer to identify. Adjusting fire on this base point enabled the Forward Observer to give fire commands to the gun position by "sensing" the distance of the target from the base point. The executive could then translate this into fire commands for the gun crews. It was these fire commands that the troops practiced for so many hours before deployment to the South Pacific. They always started with the command "Fire mission!" followed by this established sequence:

Battery Adjust. This meant that every gun crew would accept the fire commands and be prepared to fire if and when a subsequent element in the sequence indicated that the crew should fire on the target.

Shell HE. This indicated that high explosive ammunition would be used for the mission. At this point a crew member could secure one round of HE ammunition. Other types available were WP (white phosphorous, a smoke round used primarily to adjust fire) and AP (armor piercing, used against some hardened targets).

Charge 1. Each round came with six bags of powder, so it was necessary to advise the crew on how many bags would be needed for the fire mission. The number depended primarily on the range to the target. If Charge 3, for example, was indicated, the crew would use the bags numbered 1, 2, and 3. But at this point, the crew would not cut the strings connecting the bags because the weapons that would fire the mission had not yet been designated. Each crew, however, was prepared to fire when needed.

Fuse Quick. This designation told the gun crews that the fuse did not need any adjustment by the crew because the ammunition came set on fuse quick for detonation when it struck the ground or any other object. The other setting was fuse delay, which the crew could set with a screwdriver. Later in the war, the cannon companies and the field artillery received some ammunition with a proximity fuse. This kind of round would explode above the ground. It was designed to reach troops in foxholes. If the proximity fuse failed to detonate the round in the air, it would explode when it hit the ground in the same manner as fuse quick.

From Base Deflection, Right 150. This, or any similar command, told the gunner how many millimeters to move his weapon from the original setting on the base point. The executive had calculated this from the target designation given by the Forward Observer.

Number One, One Round. This was a typical fire command when the purpose was to adjust fire on the designated target by having only one gun fire until the proper range and deflection had been determined. When that had been achieved, the command would be changed to Battery, Three Rounds, or whatever number of rounds had been requested or was deemed necessary to neutralize the target.

Elevation 410. This was the final command to have the desired weapon or weapons ready to fire. When the crew had leveled the bubbles on the gun sight to the satisfaction of the crew chief, he would signal to the executive that he was ready to fire; then the executive would give the command, and only gun number one would fire. The other gun crews would have their weapons set in the same fashion and all would be ready to accept subsequent fire commands.

The method of adjusting fire was to seek to fire one round short of the target and one round beyond it, then split the difference. This was often done with smoke ammunition, especially when the target was in a wooded area where vision of the Forward Observer might be impaired.

Direct fire by these weapons on pillboxes or other point targets was an entirely different process. When a pillbox, machine-gun nest, or other point target caused problems for the rifle troops and could not be neutralized by their weapons, the Cannon Company was frequently asked to engage the target. This process required a detailed reconnaissance to identify the target to the officer in charge, the section chief, and the gunner, then to locate a firing position and a safe route to reach the firing position.

When this was accomplished, the officer and the section chief would lead the M-7 to the firing position. The crew would load the weapon before arriving at the firing position; then the section chief would order the gunner to fire as soon as the M-7 stopped its forward movement. This is why it was essential for the gunner to identify the target as well as for the officer and the section chief. As soon as the round was fired, the driver would quickly move the M-7 to the rear to place it in defilade from the target. If the first round was not a success and the target was a heavy weapon, the M-7 could expect immediate return fire. In this kind of firing, the Cannon Company, 103rd Infantry, became so adept that it seldom needed to fire a second round. When that did occur, it was necessary to repeat the process from its beginning, usually from a slightly different firing position.

Appendix 2

Field Order for M-1 Operation

[The following is the text of the original Field Order, retyped here with original errors intact.]

DECLASSIFIED PER EXECUTIVE ORDER 12356

TOP SECRET

COPY NO. 1

CANNON COMPANY, 103D INFANTRY
APO 43

11 December 1944

Field Order For
M-1 Operation

NOTE: For paragraphs 1, 2, 4 and 5, see Field Order No. 1, Hq., 103d Inf., APO 43

3.   a.   Second Platoon, 5 LVT-A4s (attached to 3rd Battalion, 103d Infantry) will:

(1) Land at H-Hour on S-Day on Beach White Three (See Annex No. 1, operations overlay and Annex No. 5 - Wave Diagram), push rapidly forward, supporting the advance of Company "I" on the left and Company "K" on the right by engaging all enemy targets in sector of advance,

first priority being fixed emplacements.

(2) At 200 yards off shore, LVT-A4s will commence firing all weapons at beach area. After landing, fire will be brought to bear on only enemy installations or enemy troops observed.

(3) Left flank LVT will primarily engage two known enemy positions on left flank.

(4) When elements of Company "I" pivot left attacking through town, three left flank LVTs will hold the ground gained being prepared to continue the attack supporting Company "L" in its drive to the railroad and subsequent envelopment of town.

(5) After 1st phase line is obtained, two right flank LVTs will move to positions in hull defilade on left flank of Company "K" covering avenues of approach from east end of San Fabian-San Jacinto road.

(6) Upon completion by third battalion of reorganization at 1st phase line, all LVT-A4s will report to assembly area under cover in vicinity of railroad at (13.0 - 50.4), (See Operations Overlay). Platoon Leader will immediately contact CO, 2nd Bn., and prepare to support attack of 2nd Bn., in its zone of action.

(7) Platoon leader will keep company CP informed at all times Of location of guns, resultsof action, status of ammunition supply and casualties.

b. Reconnaissance Officer and Platoon Sgt, Third Platoon will land with advance detachment, regimental headquarters at H plus 18 and reconnoiter first stream line approx. 400 yards from beach for crossings for M-7s, then meet LSMs bringing in first four M-7s and lead them through route reconnoitered.

c. First Platoon, Cannon Co. (less 2nd Section) and Third Platoon, Cannon Co. (less 1st Section) will:

(1) Land on Beach White Three from LSM #9 and LSM #10 respectively at H plus 28 (See Annex No. 5 - Wave Diagram).

(2) Be met at beach by Reconnaissance Officer and Platoon Sgt, Third Platoon, who will lead them over reconnoitered route past first stream line in from beach to initial assembly area.

(3) Platoon Leader, Third Platoon will immediately contact CO, 3rd Bn. to ascertain if direct fire, point blank is needed in reducing San Fabian. If so, all vehicles will immediately bring fire on enemy installations as pointed out by CO, 3rd Bn.

(4) Reconnaissance Officer, as soon as vehicles have reached initial assembly area, with such assistance as he deems necessary, will reconnoiter route for M-7s to northeast outskirts of San Fabian.

(5) Upon completion of direct fire support in San Fabian (or if none is needed), all M-7s will be led to a battery position in northeast outskirts

of San Fabian at (14.0 - 51.3).

(6) Reconnaissance Officer will take command of the battery, laying it initially on Compass 2100 so as to provide indirect fire support for entire regimental zone of action. Platoon Leader, 1st Platoon will be responsible for establishment of an OP in the vicinity of (13.8 - 51.4) providing observation of the road and railroad to the northeast so as to give timely warning of enemy mechanized attack or counter-attack in force. In case of attack all vehicles will immediately be dispatched to repel the attack by direct fire. Platoon Leader, 3rd Platoon will be responsible for establishment of a similar OP in the vicinity of (12.8 - 49.8) with observation of road and railroad to the southwest. Reconnassance Officer will make provision for constant observation of road and railroad to the east.

(7) Platoon Leader, 1st Platoon, with observation party will establish liaison with CO, 1st Bn. and provide continuous observation for indirect fire support and advise Bn CO of availability of M-7s for direct fire. Platoon Leader, 3rd Platoon, will establish liaison in the same manner with CO, 2nd Bn.

(8) Upon arrival of 2nd Section, 1st Platoon and 1st Section, 3rd Platoon in battery position, guns will be either reorganized into two platoon batteries or the last two M-7s held under cover in readiness for direct fire missions and/or displacement forward. This decision will be made by CO, Cannon Co.

(9) Upon relief of Cannon Co from anti-mechanized defense mission by Anti-Tank Co., 103d Infantry, 1st and 3rd Platoon OPs will be closed.

(10) Reconnaissance Officer will cause constant reconnaissance to be made for routes forward for displacement and subsequent gun positions in vicinity of San Jacinto.

d.　　Second Section, 1st Platoon and 1st Section, 3rd Platoon (Two M-7s) will:

(1) Land on Beach White Three on S-Day at H plus 70 from LST 15 and LST 16 respectively (See Annex No. 5 - Wave Diagram)

(2) Be met at beach by Platoon Sgt, 3rd Platoon, who will assume command of this detachment, lead them over route which he has personally reconnoitered to company gun position reporting same to Reconnaissance Officer.

e.　　Company Headquarters Platoon, Cannon Co., will:

(1) Land on Beach White Three on S-Day at H plus 38 from APA Fayette, under command of CO, Cannon Co.

(2) Move on foot to gun position in northeast outskirts of San Fabian and establish Co CP.

(3) First Sergeant will immediately organize company head-

quarters platoon into local security perimeter around gun position.

> W. S. SMITH
> Captain, Infantry
> Commanding
>
> TOP SECRET

Appendix 3

World War II Casualties

CANNON COMPANY, 103RD INFANTRY

Killed in Action

Jesse Adams
Anthony L. Aveggio
Donald D. Berggren
Arthur T. Blaquierre

Paul A. DeMeule
Alvin Isaachsen
Leo Sperdutti
Samuel Terracina

Wounded in Action

Joseph L. Baker — returned to duty
Curtis J. Banker — returned to duty
Theodore J. Jackson — evacuated
William Kopy — evacuated
Ralph R. Koschel — returned to duty
Leroy F. Kumbier — returned to duty
Clinton F. Lee — returned to duty

Injured in the Combat Zone

Kenneth Archer — gunshot wound, accidental
William S. Berwert — burned in M-7 fire
Virgil M. Dilly — broken foot
Edward H. Roberts — burned in M-7 fire
Harrison Smith — gunshot wound, accidental

Appendix 4

USS *General Hershey* Passenger List

CANNON COMPANY, 103RD INFANTRY

Name	Rank	Home of Record
Officers		
Lee, Clinton F.	1st Lt.	Shullsburg, WI
Canjar, Leo J.	1st Lt.	Denver, CO
NCO (First Three Grades)		
Machan, Leo J.	1st Sgt.	Elberon, IA
Dilly, Virgil M.	T/Sgt.	Coleman, SD
Evrard, Warren E.	T/Sgt.	Pittsburgh, PA
Gardner, Canis O.	T/Sgt.	Washington, DC
Hof, Otto G.	T/Sgt.	Chicago, IL
Juresic, Edward W.	T/Sgt.	Joliet, IL
Kraywinkel, James D.	T/Sgt.	Bakersfield, CA
Whitaker, Delmar Q.	T/Sgt.	Rolla, MO
Beinlich, Louis G.	S/Sgt.	Glenco, IL
Kennedy, David D.	S/Sgt.	Baldwin, MI
Lewis, Marvin F.	S/Sgt.	Rochester, NY
Parkinson, George E.	S/Sgt.	Santa Monica, CA

Name	Rank	Home of Record
Troop Class		
Beck, Clyde R.	Sgt.	Clayton, GA
Bernas, Jerry J.	Sgt.	Berwyn, IL
Blalock, William H.	Sgt.	Long Beach, CA
Burns, Paul E.	Sgt.	San Francisco, CA
Cochran, Clarence A.	Sgt.	Marcellino, MO
Colee, Gus	Sgt.	Providence, RI
Davendorf, Gilbert H.	Sgt.	Syracuse, NY
Meade, Henry J., Jr.	Sgt.	Bassett, VA
Schmidt, Lee R.	Sgt.	Mt. Carroll, IL
Schomerus, Carl E.	Sgt.	Nebraska City, NE
Schoneman, Leonard W.	Sgt.	Paonia, CO
Anderson, Max H.	Tec. 4	Council Bluffs, IA
Baker, Joseph L.	Tec. 4	Allison Park, PA
Brockin, Thomas E.	Tec. 4	Donaldsonville, GA
Campbell, Donald J.	Tec. 4	New York, NY
Cass, Roy M.	Tec. 4	Pampa, TX
Cooper, Hall C.	Tec. 4	Cedartown, GA
Hamm, Floyd L.	Tec. 4	Dover, PA
Hunt, Norman H.	Tec. 4	Portersville, CA
Jones, Kermit G.	Tec. 4	Jamestown, NY
Wall, Richard A.	Tec. 4	Long Branch, NJ
Bachuss, Wallace R.	Cpl.	Savannah, TN
Bartholomew, Leroy A.	Cpl.	East Troy, WI
Bowersox, Marvin E.	Cpl.	Fort Jennings, OH
Chadwell, Joe R.	Cpl.	Omaha, NE
Dailey, Paul J.	Cpl.	Turtle Creek, PA
DePue, John N.	Cpl.	Palatine, IL
Earman, Stanley E.	Cpl.	Hershey, PA
Fisher, Keller C.	Cpl.	Ringtown, PA
Kiekhoefer, Clarence A.	Cpl.	New Richmond, WI
Laribee, George C.	Cpl.	Waterloo, NY
Rejsek, Joseph, Jr.	Cpl.	Garden City, KS
Sinerchio, Michael E.	Cpl.	Fresno, CA
Baron, Frank	Tec. 5	Berwick, PA
Berwert, William S.	Tec. 5	Topeka, KS
Boydston, James F.	Tec. 5	Pawnee City, NE
Bruha, Bernard J.	Tec. 5	Hillsboro, WI
Callahan, Willilam J.	Tec. 5	Rochester, NY

Name	Rank	Home of Record
Cannady, Robert A.	Tec. 5	Belleville, IL
Crossman, Kenneth O.	Tec. 5	Fall River, WI
Hovdenes, Harold W.	Tec. 5	Sioux Falls, SD
Liebsack, George	Tec. 5	Osmond, NE
Lopez, Arthur	Tec. 5	San Pedro, CA
Norton, Ernest T.	Tec. 5	Olean, NY
Osornio, Robert	Tec. 5	San Pedro, CA
Sutton, Herman J.	Tec. 5	Huntsville, AL
White, Emitt W.	Tec. 5	Gainesville, GA
Anderson, Harvey J.	PFC	Great Falls, MT
Austin, James W.	PFC	Schuyler Falls, NY
Baldwin, Roy I.	PFC	Nevada, MO
Banker, Curtis J.	PFC	Schuyler Falls, NY
Bernas, Stanley A.	PFC	Buffalo, NY
Black,Clifford C.	PFC	Erin, TN
Bleich, Lawson E.	PFC	Buckley, IL
Bleich, Raymond D.	PFC	Buckley, IL
Brashears, Dorris S.	PFC	Cornersville, TN
Buchanan, J. W.	PFC	Waverly, TN
Butcher, Carl D.	PFC	Minneapolis, KS
Dumont, Alphonse	PFC	Bitterford, ME
Durham, James O.	PFC	Kenley, NC
Ewankiewicz, Matty P.	PFC	Union City, CA
Foote, Wayland I., Jr.	PFC	Uleta, FL
Frost, Vernon H.	PFC	Red Creek, NY
Gettis, George T.	PFC	Highland Park, MI
Gregory, Wallace	PFC	Chester, SC
Groth, Leene, E.	PFC	Los Angeles, CA
Henry, James J.	PFC	Dorothy, WV
Hobbs, Willy J., Jr.	PFC	Emporia, VA
Kersten, Fred O.	PFC	Palatine, IL
Koschel, Ralph R.	PFC	Newport News, VA
Kumbier, Leroy F.	PFC	Kimberly, WI
Matthews, James	PFC	Mt. Airy, NC
Potter, Luther M.	PFC	Danville, VA
Qualio, Angelo J.	PFC	East Hammond, IN
Roberts, Edward H.	PFC	Hulett, WY
Ruyle, Willie R.	PFC	McKinney, TX
Varela, Antonio G.	PFC	Pecos, NM

Name	Rank	Home of Record
Wisner, Ernest T.	PFC	Galena, KS
Heath, Woodrow W.	Pvt.	Grimesland, NC

Appendix 5

1993 Roster

Name of Veteran	Current Home Town	Spouse
Abilez, Alifonso	San Antonio, TX	Maria
Acosta, Julio S.	Ft. Stockton, TX	Maria
Archer, Kenneth	Las Vegas, NV	
Austin, James W.	Fulton, NY	Jerry
Bachuss, Wallace R.	Savannah, TN	Odette
Baker, Joseph L.	Lower Burrell, PA	Dora
Banker, Curtis J.	Schuyler Falls, NY	Dorothy
Bartholomew, Leroy A.	Waukesha, WI	Madeline
Beinlich, Louis G.	Northbrook, IL	
Bernas, Jerry J.	Romeoville, IL	Nancy
Bleich, Raymond D.	Paxton, IL	
Buchanan, J. W.	Waverly, TN	Mabel
Campbell, Donald J.	Brooklyn, NY	Harriet
Canjar, Leo J.	Denver, CO	Mary
Cannady, Robert A.	New Port Richey, FL	Louise
Chadwell, Joe R.	Omaha, NE	
Chea, Frank	Berwick, PA	Arlene
Cochran, Clarence L.	Iola, KS	Mary Ann

Name of Veteran	Current Home Town	Spouse
Cook, Dean W.	Monmouth, IL	Vera
Crossman, Kenneth O.	Fall River, WI	Ruby
Dailey, Paul J.	Pitcairn, PA	Ruth
DePue, John N.	Barrington, IL	Emma
Dilbeck, Chester L.	Taylorville, IL	Lucille
Durham, James O.	Edmonston, MD	Eloise
Earman, Stanley E.	Metuchen, NJ	Mary
Epperson, Guy A.	Kansas City, MO	Doris
Gagliano, Vincent	Elmhurst, IL	Jean
Hamm, Floyd L.	Manchester, PA	Jerry
Heath, Woodrow W.	Greenville, NC	Clara
Henry, James J.	Milton, WV	Daisy
Hovdenes, Harold W.	Lewisville, TX	Lois
Jackson, Theodore J.	Latham, NY	Vera
Juresic, Edward W.	Chicago, IL	
Kennedy, David D.	Muskegon, MI	
Lee, Clinton F.	Vero Beach, FL	Verda
Liebsack, George	Osmond, NE	
Machan, Leo J.	Elberon, IA	Ruth
Nelson, Kenneth W.	Moline, IL	Alice
Patterson, Harry C.	Freehold, NJ	
Ratliff, Jewell E.	Kansas City, MO	
Schmidt, Lee R.	Savanna, IL	
Schomerus, Carl E.	Nebraska City, NE	
Sinerchio, Michael E.	Fresno, CA	Emma
Smisek, Milo	Wilbur, NE	Adela
Smith, Harrison G.	Batesville, AR	
Smith, W. Stanford	Satellite Beach, FL	Martha
Waldhier, Clarence B.	Sycamore, IL	Olga
Williams, Chester A.	Fleetwood, PA	

Index

by Lori L. Daniel

Tokyo Rose, 22, 45
TPA, 4

— U —

United States, ix, 4, 22, 30, 32, 65-67, 73
   Army, ix, xi, 1-2, 4, 11-13, 17, 25, 43, 63-64, 67
   Army Reserve, 78
   Department of Commerce, 77
   Merchant Marine, 20
   National Guard, xi
   Navy, 19, 36, 44-45, 48, 59, 65
   War Department, 13
USO girls, 66
USS
   Dade, 62
   General Hershey, 63-65
   Kenton, 65
   Tryon, 24
   Shanks, 34

— V —

Vermont, xi

Veteran's Administration, 39
Vietnam, 77-78
V-mail letter, 28

— W —

Wack Wack Country Club, 53
Waldhier, Clarence B., 2, 17, 20, 70
Wall, Richard A., 2
Washington
   Fort Lewis, 1
   Seattle, 1, 65
Washington, D.C., 13
   Pentagon, 78
Weis, L. J., 39
Welch, _____, 50
West Point, 25
Wing, Leonard, 34, 40, 65-66, 76
Wisconsin
   Madison, 77
World War II, ix, xi, 67, 72, 78